D1233231

THE ART OF WESTERN RIDING

THE ART OF
WESTERN RIDING

BOB MAYHEW WITH JOHN BIRDSALL

Howell Book House 1990

REMOVED FROM COLLECTION
1771

WEST ISLIP PUBLIC LIBRARY
3 HIGBIE LANE
WEST ISLIP, NEW YORK 11795

First published in Great Britain in 1989 by The Crowood Press

© 1989 by Bob Mayhew and David Birdsall
First American Edition, 1990

All rights reserved. No part of this publication may be reproduced or
transmitted in any form or by any means, electronic or mechanical,
including photocopying, recording or any information storage and
retrieval system without permission in writing from the publishers.

ISBN 0-87605-886-1

Photographs by Vaughan Willcox except where otherwise indicated.
Line drawings by Elaine How.

Macmillan books are available at special discounts for bulk purchases
for sales promotions, premiums, fund-raising, or educational use.
For details contact:
    Special Sales Director
    Macmillan Publishing Company
    866 Third Avenue
    New York, NY 10022

10 9 8 7 6 5 4 3 2 1

Printed in Great Britain by Redwood Burn Ltd, Trowbridge

Contents

Foreword

I first saw Bob Mayhew several years ago when I was in England to judge an AQHA Breed Show. When it came time for the Reining, several runs were made, all with average scores; then, this fellow came in and after the completion of his pattern, I remarked to the ring steward that his pattern was the most correct I had seen for some time. He won the Reining handily. Two days later I met Bob and Sheila in Malvern, where I was taken to conduct a two-day clinic.

Riding Western is taken rather for granted in the United States; however, in England it was just getting started and I have never seen anyone so dedicated to its promotion. I was so impressed with Bob's enthusiasm that I returned to England the following year to help with two more clinics, one at the Avenue Riding Centre. After reading Bob's book, *The Art of Western Riding*, I was most impressed with the depth, yet also its attention to the basic breaking of the horse. I have always contended that whatever level of participation you wish to attain, no matter what event you wish to specialise in, first you must have a 'broken' horse.

My hat is off to you, Bob. Your book is excellent.

Mike Perkins
Owasso, Oklahoma

7

Acknowledgements

Few of us ever take time out from whatever we are doing to analyse what we have done and, just as important, to consider who has helped us to do it. When John came down to The Avenue Riding Centre to discuss writing this book, however, I had the opportunity to take that time out and to consider the tremendous support I have been given in my efforts to promote and expand the discipline of Western riding.

Thanks are due to my wife Sheila, my family and my friends who have all accepted, or at least tolerated, my passion for Western riding and supported me unfailingly. My wife, in particular, has had to cope with the disappointments and failures as well as all the triumphs and successes that have befallen us along the way. And I know there have been times during the endless round of demonstrations and my ceaseless search for perfection when she felt she would have received more attention and better treatment if she had been a Reining horse. But without Sheila I would never even have taken the first step on the journey that has led me so far.

Then there are the American trainers and judges who have helped me over the years and become good friends in the process. To Mike Perkins, Jim Heird, Morgan Lybbert and Dick Pieper I owe a far greater debt than I could ever hope to repay. Without their help I would never have come this far, and I would really like to dedicate this book to all of them as a token of my sincerest thanks.

But if I had to single out one person who, above all others, made this book possible, it would be the man who, when he first saw me ride with a group of other Western riding enthusiasts, thought it was the most ridiculous thing he had ever witnessed. Fortunately, he had the foresight to see that we honestly wanted to improve, to learn more and to win through against all the odds. So he persevered with us, he gave us a programme to follow and promised to return two years later to see the result. When he did, he could not believe the improvement. He loved the fact that we had got down to work, and that we were not going to allow him or anyone else to call us ridiculous again.

So I dedicate this book to the man who spurred me on along the road that has finally led me here: Pete Bowling.

Introduction

The twentieth century has been a remarkable period for both people and horses. In the early 1900s the horse held an apparently unassailable position the world over, as both a harnessable source of power and a means of transport. In a few short decades, however, its role was almost entirely usurped by steam- and petrol-powered engines. The horse population crashed. Certain breeds, such as the mighty Shire, even teetered precariously on the brink of extinction. Only in the very poorest parts of the world, or in areas beyond the reach of road and rail, did the horse continue to earn its living as it had done for centuries.

If few horsemen foresaw that rapid demise, however, fewer still would have predicted the horse's recovery. For, today, the horse population is actually greater than at any time in history. This current return to popularity has not been brought about by any reappraisal of the horse's economic value. Instead, the horse has been transformed from a beast of burden to a beast of leisure. People everywhere are discovering that the unique partnership between horse and rider provides the perfect antidote to the stresses and strains of the mechanical modern world. As a result, all forms of equestrian activity, from showing to show jumping, have seen a dramatic increase in popularity.

One result of all this new-found popularity is that many newcomers, who have had no previous connection with horses whatsoever, are now being attracted to riding. Many live in cities and are quite divorced from the traditions of the local hunt or point to point. For these new converts, often their first contact with horses is a holiday trail ride or pony trek.

Filled with enthusiasm to learn more about horses and riding, for many the next step is a trip to their local riding school. Most riding schools teach riding in much the same way, schooling the rider in the classical or English style and following in the jumping and hunting tradition. For many riders, and particularly the older ones, this 'one style fits all' approach to riding can prove a very frustrating experience indeed.

Western riding, on the other hand, is a style of riding that has something to offer everyone. Whether you simply want to enjoy the occasional hack in perfect safety, compete in the many and varied Western competition classes, or apply some of the special techniques to sharpen your show jumping or dressage form, Western schooling has something to offer you.

My fascination with the art of Western riding began the moment I first saw a well-schooled Western horse ridden by a competent rider. As I watched how softly and obediently the horse worked, responding to aids I could barely detect, I knew that this was the style of riding for me. The greatest problem I faced at the time was finding out more. Not only was Western riding widely confused with the appalling riding demonstrated in Hollywood westerns, but Western, as opposed to English riding, has tended to be regarded as simply something one did. The longer you did it the better you got at it. No one seemed to regard it as worthy of serious study or analysis, and much of its lore was passed by word of mouth from one old hand to another.

Today the situation is very different, and I sincerely hope that this book will make a further contribution towards helping more riders discover the sheer pleasure of riding in a way that is controlled yet natural, precise yet relaxed. As I hope to make clear, to knock Western riding is to attack the very roots of all equestrian disciplines and is a sure indication of a lack of understanding of the art of horsemanship!

The first and most widely held misconception is that Western riding is accurately portrayed by the TV/movie image of cowboys and rodeos. Nothing could be further from the truth. The training methods and riding style of the true art bear no relationship whatsoever to the mauling meted out to horses by Hollywood heroes, whether good guys or bad. And just as no right-minded anthropologist would take a blind bit of notice of Hollywood's history of the American Indian, so no one should believe that anything useful can be learned about Western riding from the way horses are spurred across the silver screen.

The second most commonly held prejudice concerning Western riding is the belief that because the USA only declared its independence from Britain a little over 200 years ago, its indigenous style of horsemanship must necessarily be naive and have little of value to offer the 'classical' rider. I only wish more people knew that a three-year-old Western-trained horse can sidepass, turn on the haunches, turn on the forehand, renvers, travers and much more and still stay sound and healthy; and that novice Western riders start to learn these manoeuvres almost right away! Perhaps then Western riding would receive the wider attention it deserves.

Thankfully, these prejudices are now being overcome as a growing number of people discover the truth about this exciting style of riding. Furthermore, it is interesting to note that many riders who have mastered their own particular form of equitation, be it polo, dressage, eventing or show jumping, have been among the first to understand that Western riding has a valuable part to play in the equestrian scene.

So put aside that TV/movie cowboy image and discover what the fundamental techniques of Western riding can do for your horsemanship. The basic techniques of Western riding can benefit riders in any discipline. Above all, they can help increase your riding pleasure and your enjoyment of your athletic friend.

I hope that when you have finished this book you will be tempted to try some of the techniques for yourself. You may even become totally hooked on the whole scene of Western riding. I am certain you will become addicted to the soft, light style of riding and the enjoyment of having so much more control. You may even realise that you do not have to go hunting or show jumping to get the most from your four-legged friend.

There is one final point I would like to get straight, which I am aware may trouble some would-be Western riders, and that concerns the 'cowboy' hat. Ignoring the fact that this is perhaps one of the most practical all-weather hats ever designed, when all is said and done, it is only an accessory. Western riding is not about what you wear, it is about the quality and style of your horse's movement. Only if you enter Western show classes is Western dress required; just like the top hat and tails of dressage, what you wear at other times is up to you.

I promise you, however, that if you train your horse to an acceptable standard in any of the Western classes, you will soon be itching to get into the show ring, hat and all! For you will be so proud of your horse and your ability to perform as a team, that you will not be able to resist showing off your new-found skills.

Western riding has given me an enormous amount of pleasure over the years, so much, in fact, that I cannot resist sharing it! But if I need to offer just one more prompt to persuade you to give it a try, then ask yourself this, what do you want from your horse, and what sort of riding do you actually enjoy most?

If you like the idea of owning a horse that will be calm and relaxed to handle and light and responsive to ride, a horse that will be able to cope with the hazards and obstacles of the everyday hack on roads and tracks, and that will respond to the gentlest aid while coping with any challenge, from jumping against the clock to a dressage test, then do read on. For in the chapters to come you will find out how to produce just such a horse and so discover for yourself the pleasure that is Western riding.

1 The Way West

The style of riding that today we call Western, is instantly identified with the western frontiers of America where it developed and flourished. But its roots stretch right back across the Atlantic Ocean to the Old World, where they were originally nourished by the same thoughts and practices that gave rise to the so-called 'classical' or 'English' school of riding. So, to put Western riding into a meaningful perspective and see how it relates to other forms of equitation, it is useful to take a brief look at its history.

A quick canter through man's long association with the horse is enough to show that all the various modern schools of riding can be traced back to the same place. For the first acknowledged master of horsemanship, whose teachings still hold good today, was Xenophon, a Greek cavalry officer who lived around 400 BC.

From his writings, we know Xenophon clearly understood that by training his horses and men to a higher standard of suppleness, balance and obedience, his cavalry would have a decided advantage over their enemies. Despite two millennia of refinement, much of what he taught remains relevant today for those of us interested in using the horse for both sport and leisure. A short quotation shows just how true this is. Discussing rein contact, Xenophon offers the following advice:

The hand must be neither held so strict as to confine and make the horse uneasy, nor so loose as to not let him feel it. The moment he obeys and answers to it, yield the bridle to him. This will take off the stress and relieve his bars in confirmation of this maxim, which should never be forgot, which is to caress and reward him for whatever he does well. The moment that the rider perceives that the horse is beginning to place his head, to go lightly in hand and with ease and pleasure to himself, he should do nothing that is disagreeable, but flatter and coax and suffer him to rest awhile and do all he can to keep him in this happy temper. This will encourage and prepare him for greater undertakings.

How true that is. Today, a Western trainer will employ all these ideas in his schooling programme. Visit any reining trainer and watch him work. You will see how he constantly rewards his horses by letting them stand and 'fill up on air' after they have performed a manoeuvre well, or have taken another step up the rungs of their training ladder.

To perform the tasks demanded of it, the Western horse has to become a flexible, well-trained, balanced athlete which looks forward to its job. This can only be achieved by light guiding hands and an effective use of the seat and legs – facts that Xenophon clearly understood.

But just how did the teachings of a Greek cavalry officer, who lived over 2,000 years ago, find their way to the North American continent, where the horse had already become extinct early in its evolutionary development? In the most simplistic of terms, the art of riding was refined and passed on as successive conquering nations developed more effective ways of using horses in war.

Much of Xenophon's wisdom and insight was inherited by the various 'horselords' who used the horse as their passport to conquer much of Asia and Europe. Alexander, Attila and Genghis Khan are just three of the most successful and best-remembered warriors who won kingdoms from the back of a horse. It was the Moors, however, who finally brought their riding skills to Spain, and the Spanish *conquistadores* who exported them to the New World.

The Horse Returns to the New World

Cortez reportedly landed in the New World in 1518 with eleven stallions, five mares and one foal. It was not until 1598, however, when Juan de Onate headed north of the Rio Grande with 400 settlers, 6,000 cattle, 150 colts, 150 mares and 25 stallions, that the colonisation of North America really began.

As the colonists moved north, they drove their cattle before them. The cattle flourished on the lush plains and the vastness of the area necessitated the use of the horse to work the herds. The Spaniards' basic cavalry training provided a good foundation for this work, as it had already done on the cattle *ranchos* in Spain. Working now in much larger areas, it became even more important to soften and slow the horse's paces, while still maintaining engagement and collection. This allowed the horses to work around the cattle in a businesslike way while remaining relaxed, which was good for both horse and cattle. With not a fence between Mexico and Canada, a stampede caused by a flighty horse could have had disastrous consequences.

The long distances which were covered, and the correspondingly long days spent in the saddle also demanded an emphasis on a softness of style, so that the horse and the rider would stay sound. The more relaxed and sweeping the horse's stride could be made, the less concussion there would be on the legs and ligaments. The less concussion there was and the more level the top line remained, the smoother the ride would be.

From those early days, right up until the present, the job of the ranch or stock horse has changed little. Consequently, the aims, if not always the techniques, of the Western trainer have also remained largely the same. Historically, there developed, however, a slight divergence in styles between horsemen in California, who adhered strongly to the teachings of their Spanish forebears, and those of Texas, who borrowed more freely from the British.

The Californian Style

The Californian method was to train the horse to move with grace, lightness and suppleness in a rather bridled manner. Training would begin in a braided rawhide noseband, called a bosal, which applies pressure on the poll, nose and jaw. The bosal is used with reins, or *mecate*, made of plaited horsehair.

At first the young horse is trained with a bosal with a reasonably thick diameter core. As the horse becomes better trained, a thinner, lighter bosal is used. Only when the basic schooling is complete, and the trainer feels that the horse has total understanding of what is being asked of it, is the spade bit introduced.

While spade bits often look horrendously fierce (and are in the wrong hands) and provoke a strong reaction from many novice English riders, we must respect that the Californian trainer was doing his utmost to turn out a horse with an extremely light and sensitive mouth. He would never pull hard on a spade bit. In fact, initially the bit would simply rest in the horse's mouth with no reins attached to it at all. Then 'four reins' would be used, one pair on the spade and one pair on the bosal. At each step of the training programme, the trainer would make sure that the horse was happy and relaxed before moving on to the next, until finally he would be using the curb reins only.

The early Californians prided themselves on preserving the early Spanish training methods and principles of horsemanship, even to the extent that some of the children of the wealthier families were sent to Spain for their training.

The Texan Style

By contrast, the Texan method was to have the horse far less bridled. The trainers would start in a snaffle bit, which they originally borrowed from the British who had settled on the east coast. They would then move to a grazer bit. This is a fixed bar, short sidepiece bit which offers a lighter response than the snaffle, but is not too severe in the mouth.

In the early days, the Texans favoured practicality over style and did not seem to want the horse as 'finished' as their Californian counterparts. They used split reins instead of the closed reins of the Californians, and their saddles were slightly different in style and rigging.

Western Riding Today

Following the war with Mexico of 1846–48, many Americans from the south and east moved west, and thus an intermingling of horses, riders and styles took place. Even so, the arguments over which was the better style of horsemanship would probably still be raging if it were not for the formation of national bodies set up to monitor and regulate the various Western riding disciplines worldwide.

These bodies set universal standards and aims for all Western riders. Today, the National Snaffle Bit Association, the National Cutting Horse Association and the National Reining Horse Association, to name just three, set standards for competitors and judges worldwide. An NHRA judge will, therefore, apply the same standards whether he or she is in California, Texas or Herefordshire.

The judge will not mind whether the horse is ridden with the romal rein or split reins. Providing the horse performs the required manoeuvres with accuracy and style, it will receive due credit and be marked accordingly. That is how it should be, for, after all, there are really only two types of riding: good and bad.

The skills required to ride well have not really altered much over the past 2,400 years, especially as far as the Western rider is concerned. Today, in America and throughout the world, the Western horse is continuing to make its mark, not only as a working horse capable of negotiating land inaccessible to car or truck, but also in the show ring and out on the trail where it has proven itself to be a tremendously trainable and enjoyable horse to ride.

As a result, Western riding is a sport

that is still in touch with its roots. Show jumping and dressage have become pure sports, but many Western horses still earn their living working on a ranch. For this reason, much of their training still retains a refreshing practicality that is based on what works in reality.

The ultimate goal of any Western trainer is to produce a light, supple, obedient and athletic horse which can be ridden on an extremely light contact with just one hand on the reins, while willingly tackling any job its rider asks of it. Surely that was what Xenophon was saying all those years ago.

This emphasis on training the horse underpins the whole approach I have taken with this book. It should always be your aim to produce the horse first. Certainly, there are fundamental basics of riding technique which must also be learnt. But knowing how to produce your horse, knowing what your goal is, is far more important. For it is that knowledge that makes a good horse look great, and even a bad horse look good. It has been proved many times, in all equestrian disciplines, that a person sitting on top of a horse, looking pretty but totally lacking in feel and understanding of how to produce the horse, will soon result in a decline of the horse's ability.

It is the skill, tact, feel and understanding of the rider that brings the partnership to life. And let us make no secret of it, the joy of riding is bringing that partnership to the highest level possible, whichever type of saddle and style of riding you happen to prefer.

2 A Way of Going

For many riders, their love of horses can be traced back to the first time they saw a frisky youngster showing off in a field. The sight of a colt kicking up its heels and then cantering full tilt at the gate, only to stop inches short, turn on a sixpence and nonchalantly trot away with his tail held high, is quite irresistible. What makes such a display so appealing is the unique way the horse combines grace and power in equal measures.

Unfortunately, all too often, once a rider climbs aboard, all the horse's natural poise is lost. If you can understand why this happens, however, you can begin to appreciate the part the rider must play in this new partnership. Only by understanding how your horse moves and how you may influence this motion will you be able to get the best from it, whether you are simply hacking down a country lane or racing against the clock in a jump off.

If I had to sum up Western riding in the fewest words possible, I would describe it as a way of riding lightly, so that both horse and rider move together softly and in harmony. With those thoughts in mind, it is clear that before you can begin to consider the qualities of the ideal Western horse and how it should be ridden, you must first understand a little about the way a horse stands and the mechanics of the horse in motion.

The Mechanics of Motion

I realise that the phrase 'the mechanics of motion' sounds rather daunting. Do not be put off. All I am talking about here is how and why a horse moves the way it does, so that you will understand better how you can influence it when you are riding.

Movement is all about the losing and regaining of balance. If you view a horse from the side at the halt, you can see that its natural point of balance lies just behind the withers. If you were strong enough, you could place a hand under this point and lift the horse straight up.

If, however, you drew a line across the horse at a point nearer to where you would sit, you can see that, while standing, the horse carries about 60 per cent of its weight on the forelegs and 40 per cent on the hindlegs.

It should also be obvious that if the horse lowers its head and neck, its point of balance will move forwards. If it is not to fall on its nose, it must then move its legs under it to shift its point of balance back and so regain its equilibrium. From this you can see at once that forward motion is achieved by more than just the propulsion of the rear legs. It is a constant losing and regaining of balance.

If you are still in any doubt about this, you can easily prove it to yourself. Stand up straight with your legs together, and then lean forward. If you do not want to fall over, you will have to move a leg underneath yourself to regain your bal-

Fig 1 The centre of balance of the horse.

ance. Repeat the process and you will be walking. Do it faster and you will end up running.

From the moment the young foal takes its first steps it is learning about balance. At first the young, green horse will rely heavily on its head and neck as balancing aids – just as a child might use its arms. But sooner or later the young horse will learn to engage its hocks a little more and so move its centre of balance rearwards, lightening the forehand independently of the head position.

As soon as you climb up on your horse's back, however, you alter its balance once again, and it must relearn these lessons. At first it will move a little awkwardly, rebalancing itself with its head and neck just as it did when it was a foal. You can help to teach your horse to move its centre of gravity back by bringing its hocks further under it and engaging deeper and so staying balanced while maintaining the correct head carriage.

From this it is easy to see how the position of the rider can influence the horse's balance. For example, a rider leaning forward will obviously move the horse's centre of gravity forward. This may actually be the rider's intention, as in racing when the rider helps the horse to move quickly by aiding the forward loss of balance.

On the other hand, the Western horse and rider need to be a balanced unit that is light on the forehand and so able to perform the variety of tasks demanded of it. It

Fig 2   A good position with shoulder, hip and the back of the heel in line; heels down, knee flexed. Sheila should be looking up a little more.

21

Fig 3   The wrong position, caused by the rider trying to force her heels down. This allows the lower leg to drift forward and makes the pelvis rotate. This puts the rider behind the centre of gravity and on her buttocks – commonly called 'riding the cantle' or the 'farmer's hunt seat'!

is important therefore that you learn to sit in a position whereby you are in control of your balance at all times. Just as in the trick where the magician whips away the table cloth to leave all the crockery in place, so you too should always be in a position whereby, if the horse was magicked away from under you, you would land upright on your feet in a balanced position.

I feel that the correct riding position is easier to understand if you think not of sitting on a saddle, but of standing in it, with your knees bent. In order to do this your shoulder, hip and heel must be in line. Let me stress that this position has nothing to do with looking pretty, but everything to do with staying in balance and harmony with your horse.

The Horse in Motion

With the odd exception or two, horses are capable of four distinct ways of moving, which are called gaits. These are the walk, trot, canter and gallop. As far as our training programme is concerned, we are only interested in the first three. Each gait is distinguished by a different sequence of leg movements. By understanding these sequences, later on in the schooling programme you will find it easier to influence your horse's speed and direction. If you always make things easy for your horse, it will learn more readily and happily.

The Walk

The walk is a four-beat gait, so-called because the horse moves each of its legs individually in four separate movements. If you watch a horse walk, you will see that this is a very active gait, with a lot going on at once. This is because the horse has to keep adjusting its balance, for at walk it is moving both legs on one side followed by both legs on the other. (*See* Fig 4.)

Depending on which leg you see move first, you might think that the walk is a diagonal pattern of leg movements. But if you keep watching, you will see that the sequence is left rear, left front, right rear, right front, left rear again and so on.

A horse that is walking correctly should look bright and alert and be responsive to the guidance of the rider. All four feet must touch the ground at different times and each foot should come up out of the ground at the same pace as it went in. The ideal walk is flat, ground-covering, soft and comfortable for both horse and rider.

The Trot and Jog

At the trot the horse moves its legs diagonally, and in pairs. This makes the trot a two-beat gait, because first one pair of legs is moved forwards followed by the other pair and so on (eg. left hind and right fore, right hind and left fore). Because a diagonal pair of legs is always on the ground, the horse is always well supported and well balanced at the trot, although the novice rider, sitting on a trotting horse for the first time, might not agree. (*See* Fig 6.)

This fact is borne out, however, by the relative stillness of the horse's head at the trot, which should be matched by the rider's hands for a more constant and even rein contact. The Western jog is basically a slow trot. It is still a two-beat gait, but now the horse should have a little less knee and hock action and

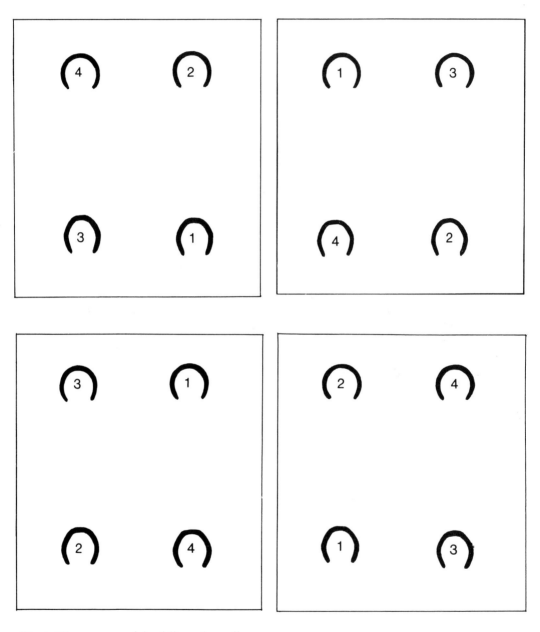

Fig 4 The sequence of footfalls at the walk.

*Fig 5   Our four-year-old nicely relaxed but just a touch
on the forehand – showing his inexperience.*

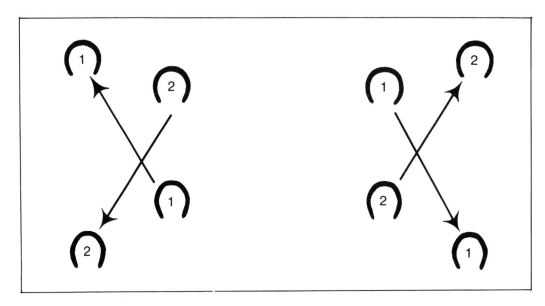

Fig 6 *The sequence of the legs in trot.*

Fig 7 *A balanced jog for a young horse – light contact, almost level topline, soft stride.*

Fig 8 A nicely balanced jog. The rider is in show ring dress.

shorten its stride. These changes create a pace that is both slower and more comfortable to sit to.

The ideal jog is nicely defined by the National Snaffle Bit Association as:

A distinct two-beat gait with a hind foot and a diagonal front foot hitting the ground at the same time. The hocks are well under and the front legs are reaching out. If you watch a horse trotting in slow motion, you can see the smooth rhythm of this two-beat gait and how the horse lifts its back and is suspended in the air momentarily as its legs are swept underneath. A good jog must have this lift which produces a clean, soft, sweeping, up and down motion.

The Canter and Lope

The canter is a three-beat gait. The two legs of one diagonal pair are moved individually, while the other diagonal pair is moved together. In the canter the foreleg which moves on its own is said to be the leading leg. The horse moves into canter off its outside rear; it then moves the opposite diagonal pair of legs together and completes the gait with its inside foreleg (e.g. right hind, left hind and right fore, left fore).

From this it can be seen that as the horse moves forward, it is balanced for two beats on just one leg and for one beat on two. It is also possible to appreciate how differently a horse balances itself

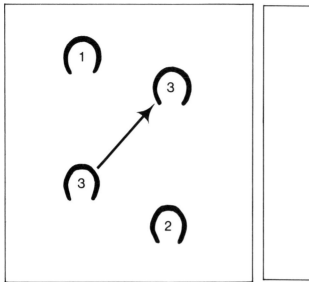
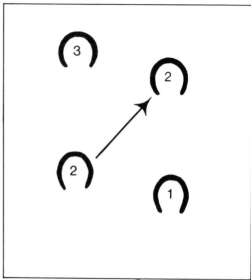

Fig 9 *The sequence of the legs in canter.*

Fig 10 *At canter: the young horse showing the lift in the back that the rider must absorb through a soft lower back and pelvis.*

Fig 11 A three-year-old Quarter Horse showing a free-moving canter in the capable hands of trainer David Deptford. The horse is relaxed and alert, and David is using only light, guiding hands.

when leading with its inside foreleg as opposed to its outside foreleg. It is this difference in balance that dictates which lead is most comfortable for a horse when it canters to the left or right. If you watch how uncomfortable a horse looks cantering a circle on the 'wrong' lead, you can begin to appreciate how important it is to recognise which lead your horse is taking each time you canter. (*See* Fig 9.)

The lope is basically a slow canter. Here not only is the stride shortened, but the speed of each stride is slowed too. This softens the gait but increases the time the horse spends on one leg. To maintain its balance, the novice horse must use its head and neck even more, increasing the 'rocking horse' appearance of the gait.

The NSBA sums up the lope as follows:

The lope is a rolling three-beat gait. The horse's legs are sweeping and moving freely. The count of the three-beat lope is not an evenly spaced 1-2-3. There is a slight hesitation after the first stride to give a 1, 2-3, 1, 2-3, rhythm.

The count of a three-beat lope begins as the drive foot hits the ground, the off fore and lead hind foot, which then strike the ground at almost the same time, make the two beat. The third beat is added when the lead fore leg strikes the ground.

At the lope the horse should be providing the rider with a comfortable natural rolling motion. This is established by the horse's lift in the body and back. The graceful lift in the horse's back is what makes the slight hesitation between the one and two beats.

The Gallop

The gallop is the horse's fastest pace. It is not simply a speedy, three-beat canter, but a quite distinct four-beat gait. As the cantering horse accelerates, the diagonal pair of legs moving together become disunited. In the gallop the hind leg touches down momentarily before the foreleg. This gives the fourth beat and the sequence: right rear, left rear, right fore, left fore.

With the possible exception of the run

Fig 12   The sequence of legs at gallop.

down to a sliding stop, the gallop has little practical use in the Western riding disciplines discussed here.

The Quality of Motion

Whatever gait you are in, it is the quality of motion that is important. Again, this quality is succinctly defined by the NSBA.

In all gaits a good mover travels best under light control without intimidation. The horse must not show fear of forward motion either by lifting its head or by its head being behind the vertical, both are signs of intimidation which can also cause excessive slowness. The fearful horse loses confidence and will often hold back because it is frightened to move forward. It will often just 'go through the motions' or drag its toes.

In extreme cases an intimidated horse may become so heavy on the forehand that it stumbles. The horse may also become inattentive and drift about. Another fault is a horse that short steps behind the trot, reaching with one leg but relaxing with the other. This gives a very uneven stride and the horse may even appear lame.

A horse that moves too slowly will appear to leave its feet on the ground too long. In the trot the two beat may become a four beat. Instead of trotting, the horse does a fast walk. In the lope if the horse does not use its back and achieve the necessary lift it will need more reach in front. The horse will then use too much knee and slap the ground in front. Its weight will be too far forward causing its head to bob about and it may eventually stumble. If there is not enough drive and adequate lift there will not be enough hang time for the horse to sweep the legs underneath its body in a pendulum fashion.

Engagement

A term that you will encounter frequently in this book is engagement. I have said that to move its centre of gravity back, a horse must bring its hocks underneath itself and increase 'engagement' or 'engage deeper'. This is, however, a term which many novice riders find difficult to understand. Engagement basically describes how the horse is using its hindquarters and may be applied to any gait or pace. A horse which is not engaged is said to be 'on the forehand'. This is another way of saying that because it is not getting its rear legs under it, too much of its weight is being carried by its forelegs. A horse that is on the forehand is not simply unattractive to watch; it is also unbalanced and so less able to respond nimbly to any aids the rider gives it.

An easy way to determine whether a horse is engaged or not is to imagine a line dropped from the point of the buttock down the back of the cannon bone to the ground. As a horse moves, its rear legs will first pass in front of this line and then fall behind it. The further it brings its legs under it and in front of the line, and the less it leaves them trailing behind the line, the more engaged it is; it is as simple as that.

The well-schooled Western horse should always show good engagement. The slower Western gaits must be achieved through greater engagement and not through slowing the horse down with the reins, or by letting it slop along on the forehand.

Turning

So far we have only considered movement in a straight line, but very little riding is actually done without a change of direction. Now you must consider how a horse changes direction. If you watch a horse turn naturally when it is out in a field, more often than not it will keep its head and neck straight or bend them to the outside. It will then drop its shoulder to the inside, rotating its barrel, and scoot round.

This technique might be fine for the loose horse, but it has a very unbalancing effect on the rider. For this reason it is necessary for you to alter your horse's natural way of turning in order for you to remain secure. You need to teach your horse to remain upright through its body, to look in the direction of the turn and to make sure its shoulders follow the nose and that the hindquarters follow the shoulders.

If you turn with the horse's head to the outside and its shoulder dropping in, you are going to encourage the horse to scramble round a turn and increase its speed. You can liken this technique to riding a bicycle. To corner quickly you have to lean into the turn. To steer round a turn keeping the bike upright, you must turn more slowly or you will fall off.

The more you watch and understand how horses move the more understanding a rider you will become. You will also begin to appreciate how the conformation of your horse can determine the quality of movement it displays. From this you will be able to assess the suitability of any particular horse for Western riding or, for that matter, for any other riding discipline.

3 Conformation

To ride Western you will quite obviously require a suitable horse. It need not be of any particular breed, but it must be suitable for the job in hand. As I have already explained, Western riding is a soft, light style of riding, demanding soft paces and good engagement. There is also an emphasis on 'handiness'. So, if you want to have any chance of success, you must work with a horse which has a suitable conformation and a willing temperament.

Some people try to present the study of 'conformation' as an arcane science, requiring years of experience before it can be fully understood. In plain English, however, conformation is simply the way a horse is built. Just as you can appreciate that a marathon runner has a very different build to a weight lifter, so it is not so difficult to look at the shape of a horse and take a guess at what it might or might not be naturally good at.

As far as the rider is concerned, as opposed to the handler or show horse breeder, the points of conformation which make a good Western horse are those which affect its performance. There has never been a perfect horse, and there probably never will be, but there are certain important qualities which your horse must have if it is to be able to perform the tasks you will require of it.

The Ideal Western Horse

When assessing the suitability of a horse for Western riding, you should bear the following points in mind. Examining the horse from the side, you should look for an overall picture of balance. First impressions can tell you a lot and these should be of a horse which has been 'put together' correctly. (*See* Fig 13.) You do not want a very leggy horse, for example, as not only might it be prone to lameness, but its centre of balance will be too high. Neither do you want a short-legged horse which drags its belly on the ground, for its gaits will be uncomfortable and its ability to turn restricted.

A useful trick, when studying the conformation of a horse, is to reduce the key dimensions of shoulder, back, hip and belly to a trapezoid. On a horse with good conformation, the length of the shoulder, the length of the back and the length of the hip should all be equal. The length of the back should be half the length of the underline, and the depth of the barrel should equal the distance from the belly to the ground. Once you have found a horse that is well balanced and nicely proportioned, you can go on to consider the more subtle points of conformation which the ideal horse should possess.

Beginning at the horse's head, the first thing you should look for is a nice soft, dark eye that is of good size and is forward facing. A soft eye is a good indicator of a calm and willing horse,

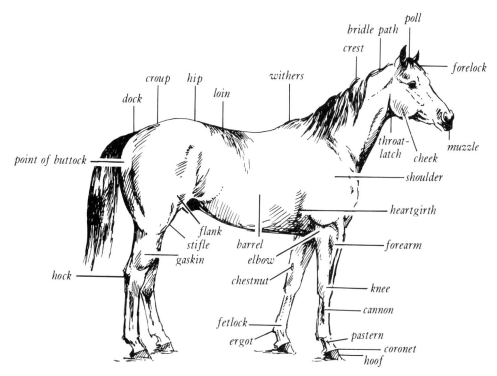

Fig 13 *The points of the American Quarter Horse horse.*
(Illustration based on artwork by Orren Mixer that is accepted
by the American Quarter Horse Association as the ideal Quarter
Horse conformation.)

while its size and position determine how good its binocular vision might be. A pig-eyed horse, with eyes on the sides of its head, is best avoided. You should also look for a nicely balanced head with a flat forehead and nose. An attractive, elegant head is another indicator of intelligence, but you also want a horse that sees, breathes and eats well. The ears should be well set on and pricked. Ears that are too long or short or laid back, suggest a horse with a poor disposition.

Moving to the neck, a good clean space between the jaw bones in the throatlatch area is important, so that the horse can flex easily at the poll. This is vital if it is to carry its head correctly and move its centre of gravity to the rear. The neck should be clean and in proportion to the body. If the neck is too long or short, the horse will find it harder to balance itself. The neck should also come out of the body cleanly, so that it can bend easily and become supple.

The shoulder should have a good slope to it. If the shoulder is too upright the horse will have a short choppy stride. At the other extreme, a horse with a very sloping shoulder will experience undue pressure and strain on its legs and tendons. This is because the slope of the shoulder is often paralleled by the slope

Fig 14 A well-made Quarter Horse stallion – four-year-old Waccabuc Skipkeo. Note the kind eye, indicating his superb temperament.

of the pasterns. A horse with a good slope to its shoulder will give a good length of stride, but with a degree of softness. This will give a softer topline and less concussion for the rider to absorb. The softer stride will also put less strain on the horse's legs and help it to stay sound.

If you take a point from the middle of the shoulder and drop a line vertically down, you should see it pass right through the centre of the foreleg and come out at the back of the heel. Clearly, if the shoulder is too upright, this line will come out in the middle of the foot.

While examining the forelegs, you should always try to avoid a horse that is over or back at the knee. As far as bone is concerned, the horse that is short in the cannon bone does not need as much bone as a horse with long cannons. The Western horse is not required to tackle very high jumps, so a lot of bone is not required. Viewed from the front, a line dropped from the point of the shoulder should pass down through the centre of the legs, the cannon bones and out through the middle of the foot.

Horses which are toed out or pigeon toed will experience extra stress on their joints and ligaments. The horse must be comfortably balanced with an even weight distribution on all four feet if it is to remain happy and sound when in training. For this reason you should watch the horse work to see that it moves straight and does not paddle or dish.

The back should be short and flat right back to a nicely sloping croup that is not too steep or too flat. You should also look for a nice slope to the hip, as again, this will affect the stride length. A nice slope will allow the horse to move its hocks underneath itself and so help you in your attempts to move its centre of gravity back when you ride it.

At the buttocks you should, again, be able to drop a vertical line downwards to pass straight through the back of the cannon bone. If the horse's legs are behind this line, you know that there will be additional strain on them and that the horse will have difficulty in getting its legs under it. Looking from the rear of the hindlegs, a line dropped from the point of the buttock should pass through the centre of the leg. A sickle-hocked horse is likely to have too much strain on the back of the hocks and so should be avoided if possible.

The cow-hocked horse may also experience leg strain. If the hocks are closer together than the lower leg then it is a true cow-hocked horse. If the gap at the hocks and fetlocks is the same, however, then the problem is not so serious, for the lower leg is still carrying weight in the correct manner. While examining the hocks you should look for a reasonable degree of angulation and avoid a horse that is too straight or too bent.

The ideal Western horse stands between 14.2hh and 15.3hh. This size makes for ease of mounting, riding and dismounting. Smaller and larger horses can also be successful, however. The type of riding you wish to do is obviously important here, so, again, it is wise to establish the purpose of your horse before becoming too concerned about its height.

From a thorough study of a horse's conformation you can learn a lot about its general disposition and how it is likely to perform. As the saying goes, however, 'a horse will make a liar out of anyone'. So be sure to watch carefully how it moves at the different gaits and how it stops and turns.

The ideal Western horse should move freely with an action that is close to the ground. It should have the ability to pick its feet up and move softly. A horse with an elevated knee or hock action will be more uncomfortable to ride. It is also possible that it may be difficult to keep sound as it will suffer a lot more concussion when each foot strikes the ground.

The low action has to be natural, however. Furthermore, it is important that while the action is low and soft, the horse must be fully engaged. If you have a horse that moves low to the ground because it has a lazy action, then the chances are that the moment you ask it to work, it will either stumble or start lifting its knees and slapping the ground with its feet.

A horse that simply loses all its motion out of the front door, or is slowed only with the reins, will move sloppily. To move cleanly at a slower pace, the horse must be more engaged and encouraged to take shorter, softer strides.

Your Horse

If you already own a horse then by now you should have a good idea how well suited it is to Western riding. Remember, though, that all horses are compromises to some extent and certain characteristics are far more important than others. A good temperament, for example, is vital.

Even the most perfectly conformed horse is next to worthless if it lacks the intelligence or the aptitude to be trained.

Never lose sight of the fact that you ride for pleasure. It is easy to become obsessed with perfect conformation, breeding and bloodlines, but at the end of the day your horse must be your friend and someone you look forward to being with. So if your horse is a 'Heinz 57' that does not quite measure up to the ideal, do not despair. Accept its faults as challenges to be overcome. Avoid asking it directly to do things it finds difficult; instead help it to work around such problems. You can still get a lot of pleasure from working together, and it may yet surprise you with abilities you never suspected it had.

If, on the other hand, you are considering buying a horse specifically to ride Western, then you should try to find a horse that meets as many of the above criteria as possible. Again, I would stress that the breed is not important, a good-value pony crossed Thoroughbred might make an ideal all rounder. You must consider first, however, which of the Western disciplines interests you most, as well as how competitively you want to take your riding. Just as in any other branch of riding, there are horses for courses, winners and also-rans.

For the rider keen to pursue Western riding to the very highest level, however, there will be no substitute for one of the genuine American breeds which, on the whole, have been bred specially to meet the demands of the Western rider.

4 Suitable Breeds

When choosing a suitable Western horse it is vital that you concentrate on type rather than breed. Even the Quarter Horse, arguably the most ideal Western breed, has also been bred for both showing and racing, producing specialists that may not meet all our requirements. Other American breeds, such as the Appaloosa, Palomino and Pinto, have standards which emphasise colour rather than conformation. For this reason, in other parts of the world these horses are regarded not as breeds but as 'types'.

With the growth in the popularity of Western riding, more useful riding horses are being bred every year. Furthermore, many of the coloured horses are being crossed back to Quarter Horse stallions to produce excellent Western mounts. I have already mentioned the importance of temperament and this cannot be over-emphasised. The ideal Western horse must be calm, sensible and trustworthy. Above all, the Western horse is a family horse. Its conformation and disposition should make it as ideal a mount for a fourteen-year-old novice as for his or her fourteen-stone (90 kg) father.

The American Quarter Horse

If there is one breed of horse which most closely matches up to our ideal of the perfectly conformed Western horse, then it is undoubtedly the American Quarter Horse. It has the largest equine registry in the world and it is arguably the most versatile of all breeds. This was the first truly American breed, created from a unique fusion of the Arabian-influenced Spanish horses and the English Thoroughbred.

The horses which the Spanish *conquistadores* brought with them to America were predominantly Barbs, hot-blooded and powerful. Over time many of these horses were sold, stolen or lost. It was not long before many found their way into Indian hands. Through indiscriminate breeding, these horses diminished in size, but became tougher and better able to fend for themselves in a harsh environment.

Of all the Indian tribes which acquired horses, the Chickasaws of Carolina were best known for their large herds. It was with the Chickasaw ponies that the new English settlers crossed their horses. This was the birth of the Quarter Horse. It still required further refinement, but its key qualities of speed and hardiness were laid on these foundations.

In the early seventeenth century, these horses were bred selectively for the increasingly popular pursuit of quarter-mile racing. Further introductions of Thoroughbred blood enhanced the breed's natural speed and soon these new 'quarter-mile horses', or Quarter Horses as they came to be known, were the fastest sprinters in the American horse world. Yet the breed retained its original quality of a relaxed self-reliance, hence its oft-quoted description as a 'sleepy little critter that can unwind like lightning'.

37

Fig 15   American Quarter Horse, 'Bozo Bouncer'. (Photograph by kind permission of the Equestrian Services, Thorney.)

Today these horses are still raced over the eponymous quarter mile, and still people gamble on the outcome. So much so that the world's richest race is not the Prix de L'Arc de Triomphe, the Grand National nor the Kentucky Derby, but the All American Futurity, contested between three-year-old Quarter Horses.

While racing provided the stimulus which established the breed, the Quarter Horse really found its niche off the turf and under a stock saddle. This fast, agile horse, with its quiet disposition and ability to withstand the harshest conditions, proved ideal as a hard-working ranch horse. Despite often standing barely 15hh, this muscular horse could easily carry a man all day and still turn on a burst of speed to run down an errant steer.

Nowadays, the Quarter Horse is proving its versatility once again as a sports and pleasure horse. Pure and part-bred Quarter Horses can be found competing successfully in every equestrian discipline from show jumping to dressage, and as the ideal Western mount, the Quarter Horse has no rival. A look at the official American Quarter Horse Association conformation standard shows just how close this breed matches up to the ideal outlined in Chapter 3.

Fig 16   American Quarter Horse, 'C.P. Lynxette'.

Quarter Horse Conformation

The head of the Quarter Horse reflects alert intelligence. This is due to his short, broad head, topped by little 'fox ears' and by his wide set, kind eyes and large, sensitive nostrils, short muzzle and firm mouth. Well developed jaws give the impression of great strength.

The head of the Quarter Horse joins the neck at a near 45-degree angle, with a distinct space between jaw-bone and neck muscles, to allow him to work with his head down and not restrict his breathing. The medium length, slightly arched, full neck blends into sloping shoulders.

The Quarter Horse's unusually good saddle back is created by his medium-high but sharp withers, extending well back and combining with his deep sloping shoulders, so that the saddle is held in the proper position for a balanced action.

The Quarter Horse is deep and broad chested, as indicated by his great heart girth and wide-set forelegs which blend into his shoulders. The smooth joints and very short cannons are set on clean fetlocks and the medium length pasterns are supported by sound feet. The powerfully muscled forearm tapers to the knee, whether viewed from the front or back.

The short saddle back of the Quarter Horse is characterised by being close coupled and especially full and powerful across the kidney. The barrel is formed by deep well-sprung ribs back to the hip joints, and the underline comes back straight to the flank.

The rear quarters are broad, deep and heavy, viewed from either side or rear, and are muscled so they are full through the thigh, stifle and gaskin and down the hock. The hind leg is muscled inside and out, the whole indicating the great driving power the Quarter Horse possesses. When viewed from the rear there is great width, extending evenly from top to bottom of the stifle and gaskin. The hocks are wide, deep, straight and clean.

39

Fig 17   American Quarter Horse, 'Miss Star Freight'. (Photograph by kind permission of the Equestrian Services, Thorney.)

The flat, clean flinty bones are free from fleshiness and puffs but still show much substance. The foot should be well rounded and roomy, with an especially deep open heel.

The Quarter Horse normally stands perfectly at ease with his legs well underneath him; this explains his ability to move quickly in any direction.

The Quarter Horse is uniquely collected in his action and turns or stops with noticeable ease and balance, with his hocks always well under him.

This outstanding conformation, combined with a bright intelligence and affection for people, bred over hundreds of years of close association, makes the Quarter Horse a riding horse *par excellence*.

The Appaloosa

The Appaloosa is arguably the oldest recognised breed of horse in the world. Cave paintings at Peche Merle, made some 28,000 years ago, show horses with the unmistakable spotted markings that characterise this unique breed. Despite

Fig 18 Appaloosa, 'Tibertich Poncho'. (Photograph by kind permission of Mrs A. Howkins.)

the great antiquity of the spotted horse, however, and its undeniable popularity as far afield as China and Europe, it is only quite recently that it has been formally recognised as a breed in its own right.

When the spotted horse arrived in North America it soon became as popular with the Indians as it had been with the nobility of Europe. The Nez Perce Indians, in particular, took to the spotted horse and bred it with care. Over centuries they selected for colour, speed, sureness of foot and a gentle, adaptable temperament. In their fertile homeland to the south east of the Palouse river, their herds of beautiful horses grew in number and reputation. So famous did they become that the spotted horse was often referred to simply as 'a Palouse horse'.

Over time this name became corrupted, but only relatively recently has the name Appaloosa been accepted for the breed.

Despite this propitious start, the North American Appaloosa was to come close to extinction. During the Indian wars of the late nineteenth century, the Nez Perce, mounted on their sure-footed and speedy spotted horses, won many a great victory over the US Army. Eventually, however, in 1877, the Nez Perce were defeated and the army wreaked a terrible revenge on the horses which had borne their enemies so successfully into battle; written orders were given to kill or destroy every Appaloosa which could be found. Even when the slaughter finally ceased, the Indians were only allowed to breed the remaining Appaloosas to draft stock, so that they could never again

41

produce such fine riding horses. The result of this purge was that a mere six decades later only a few hundred Appaloosas remained.

Reading of this horse's sorry plight in 1937, Claude Thompson, an Oregon farmer who had owned an Appaloosa when he was young, resolved to rescue the breed. He scoured America for the best breeding stock and, through careful selection and a judicious outcross to a chestnut Arab, he slowly re-established the Appaloosa as one of the most popular breeds in the world.

Appaloosa Conformation

The Appaloosa is a horse defined predominantly by colour, but it also possesses certain distinguishing characteristics which define it as a breed. These include mottled pink and black skin in the genital area and frequently around the lips, muzzle, nostrils and eyes. Appaloosas also always have a sclera (white area surrounding the iris) showing in the eye, a breed trait which should not be confused with signs of bad temper or fear. Other characteristics which are generally present, but not essential, are striped hooves, a sparse mane and tail and varnish marks. These are clumps of dark hairs which usually occur around the bridge of the nose, above the eyes, on the point of the hip, behind the elbow and on the gaskin and stifle region.

To these key breed characteristics are added eight coat patterns which may occur in any combination; consequently each Appaloosa should be quite unique in appearance. The basic patterns are the spotted blanket, white blanket, marble, leopard, near leopard, few-spotted leopard, snowflake and frosted hip.

To the characteristics and colour is added a brief breed conformation standard. This requires that Appaloosas should be hardy, sure-footed, active and extremely versatile. They should have a tractable temperament and be 'good doers'. The head should be straight and lean, and the ears pointed and of medium size. The shoulders should be long and sloping and the withers well defined. The body should be deep and the ribs well sprung. The limbs and feet should be sound and possess good bone. The action should be smooth and easy. The Appaloosa should stand 14.2hh and upwards.

The Pinto

Like the Appaloosa, the Pinto was another favourite horse of the American Indian. It, too, is defined principally by colour, being either skewbald or piebald. 'Pinto' actually comes from the Spanish word meaning painted. Although generally regarded as a type, in America the Pinto is considered a breed within which two coat patterns are recognised. These are the Overo and Tobiano. The Overo Pinto is principally black with large white patches, usually over the belly, legs and face. The Tobiano Pinto is principally a white horse with dark patches of any colour.

It is a lively active little horse that is still popular today. Although defined by colour rather than conformation, its wide use under Western saddles has meant that a good riding type predominates, although most Pintos remain rather small.

Fig 19   Palomino 'Kingsettle Écu'. (Photograph by kind permission of P. Russell Howell.)

The Palomino

Like the Pinto, the Palomino was once regarded purely as a colour type of any breed. Today, however, Palomino breed societies have been established in an attempt to combine the colour with an accepted standard of conformation. The colour is reputed to have originated in Spain where such horses were called Golden Isabellas, in honour of Queen Isabella. It is likely, however, that golden horses have occurred among all breeds throughout history.

The ideal colour is generally described as like that of a newly minted coin, but lighter and darker shades are permissible.

In all cases, the mane and tail should be white and the skin dark. White colouring is only permissible on the legs and face.

Other Breeds

Other breeds which are seen working under Western saddles include the American Saddle Horse, the Morgan and the Arab. The American Saddle Horse was once the mount of the US Cavalry. Officially founded by an English Thoroughbred, this once tough, speedy horse is now bred almost exclusively for the show ring where top horses display five gaits and a very showy action. This quality makes it unsuited to Western classes, where the emphasis is on soft, relaxed paces.

The Morgan horse is another American breed, derived uniquely from a single stallion, the eponymous Justin Morgan. A solid, cob-like horse, many Morgans also possess extravagant actions. Again, this makes them less than ideal as all-round Western horses.

The Arab has only recently achieved success as a Western horse. Originally entered in show versatility classes, an increasing number of enthusiasts began working Arabs exclusively in Western tack and with success. To perform well as a Western horse, however, it is important to find an Arab which has a suitably relaxed temperament and the required soft paces.

5 Clothing and Tack

Western riding, to a far greater extent than other equestrian styles, has given rise to a booming fashion industry offering everything from hats to boots. The popularity of Western clothing and accoutrements can, however, obscure the fact that Western riding is a style of riding and not simply a style of dress.

Western clothing and tack should be seen as simply the means to an end, not as an end in themselves. Just as pulling on a pair of running shoes will not make you a top sprinter, neither will putting a Western saddle on your horse turn you into a Western rider. But just as a runner needs to wear suitable kit, so too the Western rider must employ the correct equipment.

Despite their fashionable modern counterparts, Western clothing and tack have quite humble roots. They developed over hundreds of years as the gear which best helped the rider to work long days in the saddle in all conditions. The Western saddle, for example, was not invented by the cowboys of the 1860s. It has a history stretching right back to the great cavalries of Europe. Every part of it is made the way it is for a specific purpose, and derives from a time when a rider's life, and certainly his living, depended on his horsemanship and the equipment he used. The tack that we use today is the tack that worked best in the past.

Western Clothing

Outside the show ring there are no dress rules whatsoever. Safety and comfort should be your primary considerations. It is sensible, therefore, to wear a hard hat and clothing which will not restrict your movement. Jodhpurs are every bit as acceptable as a pair of blue jeans or needlecords. It is worth noting, however, that whereas a pair of jeans or cords might pinch your legs in an English saddle, they will prove quite comfortable in a Western saddle.

Well-fitting Western boots are very desirable for they are made to fit the Western stirrup, but they are not essential except in competition, and any suitable riding footwear is acceptable. But do try to avoid fashion boots or those with a high underslung or Cuban heel – a medium walking heel is best. Flat shoes or trainers should not be worn as they can slip through a Western stirrup as easily as an English one, and with equally disastrous results.

Show Ring Dress

If you decide to compete in Western riding competition classes then, as with every other equestrian activity, you will be expected to conform to the required dress code. You should make the effort to choose clothes of a colour and style that will enhance your own and your horse's appearance, and which suggest to the

Fig 20 Correct dress for Halter show classes – although our four-year-old stallion would not be in his winter coat!

happy to wear anywhere. The flowery 'rhinestone cowboy' styles are strictly for the country and western fan, and are not suitable for the Western rider. Your blouse or shirt should be fastened at the neck and finished off with a neat small scarf tie.

On your legs you should wear a clean pair of jeans or similar trousers; for ladies an 'equestrian suit' is very smart. These should be covered by a pair of clean neat chaps. Ideally, your chaps should colour match the rest of your outfit and complement the colour of your horse. Be sure that your chaps overhang the bottom of your leg when you try them on. That way they will just come over the bottom of your boot when you are in the saddle with your knees bent.

For the show ring the most acceptable chaps are the suede 'shotgun' style which enclose the legs and have zips up the side covered by fringes. Although decorative, these fringes were originally designed to disperse water when riding in the rain. The batwing style chaps, as used by working cowboys, are only worn in cutting events and should not be worn in any other competition.

Finally, your outfit should be completed by a pair of good quality Western boots. These should be of a working style and not fancy show boots. The boot itself should be comfortable enough to be worn as everyday footwear. A little decorative stitching is acceptable, as the original idea behind the stitching on the top of the foot, called the medallion, was to add strength where creasing would occur. The fancy stitching on the shaft of the boot was again designed to give extra strength and to keep the boot upright. The height of the boot should be chosen so that its top does not snag on the fender.

judges that you have made every effort to present yourself smartly and correctly.

Beginning at the top, you should choose a good quality hat made of Durofelt or beaver fur. To wear a cheap 'kiss-me-quick' hat simply suggests to the judges that you are not taking the competition seriously and is a major let down! A good quality hat can be steamed into shape so that there is a slight dip to the front and rear of the hat. It should be regularly dusted off with a clean dry sponge, and never left to rest on its brim.

Next, you should wear a smart, well-fitted blouse or shirt. Ideally it should be plain, or have just a simple stripe or check pattern. Choose a style you would be

Fig 21 Ladies showing at Halter can wear a smart equestrian suit.

When buying boots, check that they have a full sole. A half sole may snag on the stirrup. Most American-made boots also have a steel insert under the instep to strengthen the boot and protect the foot where it bears down on the stirrup. Obviously, a good quality, all-leather boot will prove most durable. One last point to remember when buying boots is that corresponding US sizes are generally one size larger than British sizes. A correct fit is usually achieved with a boot that is a little tight to pull on. A little slip at the heel is also acceptable when the boot is new.

Spurs

I feel spurs should be included here as although they are technically tack rather than clothing, they are worn by so many show ring competitors that their use might appear compulsory. Spurs are, however, an optional extra, as they should be in all equestrian sports. Should you decide to wear them, you should choose a Western spur with sufficient weight so that it hangs correctly on your boot. Do not choose a spur that is too sharp.

The blunt star-shaped rowels of the Western spur were originally designed so that they would run free and not puncture the horse's side should the rider's leg become trapped. The extremely sharp spurs which some riders did wear were not designed to inflict pain on the horse, as this would quickly have become counter productive. They were badges of the rider's skill, proclaiming that his horse would obey the lightest aid.

Spurs should also be used by experienced riders who understand exactly when and how to apply them. It should be the goal of all riders to produce a horse that will obey the subtlest command instantly without resistance. It should be possible to ride a 'finished' horse in such a way that none of your aids is visible to onlookers. Spurs can help to achieve this end by backing up your aids in the early stages of training. All the time you are working with your horse you should be training it to move away from leg pressure. Every time you ask your horse to move you should begin with just the pressure of thigh and calf. If the horse fails to comply, you should squeeze harder. And if this still fails to have the desired effect, then, lastly, you should turn out your toe and apply the spur as a gentle prod.

Once the required response has been achieved, however, it is vital that the next time you ask for the same movement you begin again with gentle leg pressure. All too often I have seen riders kick their horses when they have failed to do what the rider wished. If the kicking succeeds in, say, urging the horse to sidepass, they then apply the logic that to make their horse move away they must kick it every time. There is no quicker way to produce a horse that is unhappy, dispirited and resistant to every aid.

Only by always giving your horse the chance to respond to the lightest aid, even if you must repeat the lesson over and over again, will you ever create a horse that is light and a pleasure to ride. Spurs can be a means to this end. They must never be seen as a means of punishment.

The Western Saddle

The saddle is the largest and clearly the most important piece of tack. It is vitally important that it should fit both horse and rider well. No amount of silverware and fancy tooling will add to the quality of the horse which wears it. A well-fitted saddle, on the other hand, will enable the horse to carry you more comfortably and so can directly affect the horse's performance by relaxing it and making it move more smoothly.

So, while it is nice to dress up a good-looking horse with smart-looking tack, it is essential that the tack fits correctly. If you do want a saddle that is a little different, shop around for something tasteful. Do not go overboard however; judges do not like to see show ring competitors riding on parade saddles sporting silver studs and *tapaderos*.

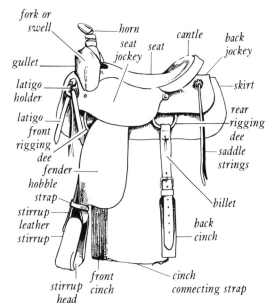

Fig 22 The parts of the Western saddle.

Fig 23 A simple working saddle.

Fig 24 A pleasure/competition saddle.

You can judge the quality of a Western saddle in much the same way as you would an English saddle. Look for good hard, close-grained leather and neat stitching. Most Western saddles are lined with imitation sheepskin, but it is still worth turning them over to see how well finished they are underneath. Although there are many superficial differences among Western saddles, there are three main types which you may come across.

The first is the plain working saddle. This type of saddle has no fancy work at all. It should be a plain straightforward saddle of good quality. If you rub the leather between your hands, its weight and feel should suggest it has been made with the rider in mind and made to last. A

working saddle usually features saddle strings, so that you can tie on accessories such as wet weather gear and small packs. It should have comfortable, flat-treaded stirrups that help to relax your feet. I like to avoid roping saddles with heavy stirrups and fenders as they are often very stiff and rather uncomfortable.

The second type of saddle you may encounter is the general purpose show saddle. This style has the same nice deep seat as the working saddle, with a gentle slope from the base of the seat to the horn. This allows the rider a little freedom to move around in the saddle. It is usually decorated with some simple hand tooling and subtle silverwork.

The third type of saddle commonly

49

Fig 25 A cutting saddle.

seen is the cutting saddle. This is the type I prefer because I like the flatter seat which gives me more freedom to move. With these saddles, however, you generally have to alter the stirrups, as cutting saddles usually have narrow, ox-bow stirrups designed to fit tightly around your instep. These are used because when a horse is cutting cattle it moves like a whip, and it is vital that the rider does not lose a stirrup or he will be on the ground in a flash. Using a cutting saddle for general purpose riding, or for reining, as I do, a flat-treaded stirrup is more comfortable and offers better balance.

Again, like the general purpose saddle, a good quality cutting saddle may feature a simple amount of tooling, silver and lacework so that it is smart but not ostentatious. The cutting saddle also usually has a higher horn.

Fitting a Western Saddle

A Western saddle of whatever design must fit the horse properly. It should fit at the withers and over the back and not rub the loins. There should be sufficient air space down the centre gullet so that the saddle stays clear of the horse's back, even with a rider on board. Just as you would fit an English saddle, you should check the fit of a Western saddle on the horse, ideally without a saddle pad at first. If any part of the gullet comes down on the spine, pinches at the withers or digs at the back, then you are in for trouble.

Western saddles may be a lot heavier than English saddles, but properly fitted they distribute the rider's weight more evenly over the horse's back. For this reason many horses actually seem to prefer, and go better under, a Western saddle.

Setting the Fenders

If you buy a new saddle or even a second-hand one which has not been used much, then you may find it rather uncomfortable until you have set the fenders. (These are the large pieces of leather which cover the stirrup leathers.) If you look at a new saddle, you will note that the stirrups appear to face inwards towards the horse. If you do not set them correctly, you will soon get sore ankles because you will be fighting against the set of the leather, which will be trying to turn your toes in.

To set the fenders, you should first oil

the saddle lightly. Then soak the back of the fenders and stirrup leathers with water. Lie the saddle down flat, with the fenders and stirrup leathers out to each side. Now take each stirrup and bend it over to one side, making a diagonal crease down the fender. Place a large weight on top of each one to hold it in position, and leave them to dry out naturally.

The fibres of the leather will stretch and stay permanently set, so that the stirrups hang in a more comfortable and natural riding position. Nearly every time I have ever heard someone say that they find a Western saddle uncomfortable I have traced the problem to the fenders not being set!

Saddling Up

Before saddling up, I always pad the horse well, with either a one-piece blanket about one inch (25mm) thick, or a pad that is made of felt or horsehair, two-thirds of an inch (15mm) thick, over which a blanket is placed. The pad should absorb sweat while still allowing the skin to breathe. Remember, everything you do should be designed to make things as comfortable as possible for the horse.

With the pad placed well up on the horse's withers, you can lift the saddle up and lower it gently into place. Do this with both hands so that you can position it carefully. Whatever you do, do not

Fig 26 Felt 'cut-back' pad.

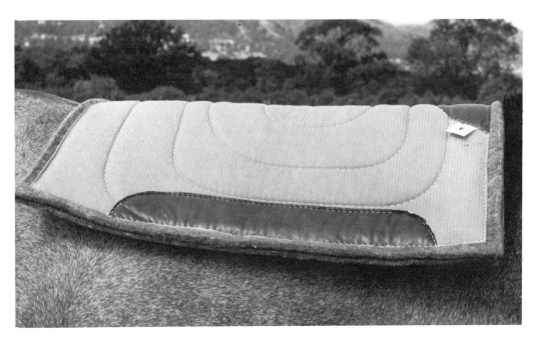

Fig 27 Combination pad/blanket.

Fig 28 Horsehair pad with duck canvas top.

Fig 29 Navaho-style blanket.

Fig 30 Standard low-cost manmade fibre blanket.

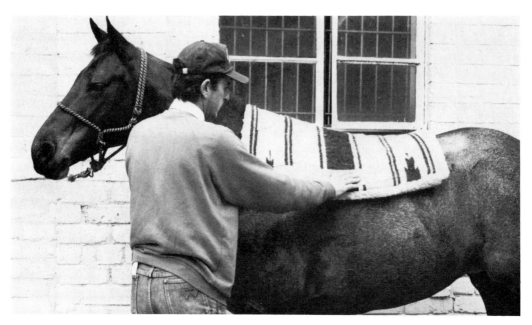

Fig 31 Tacking up: place the saddle pad well up on the withers.

Fig 32 The saddle with the stirrups neatly stowed on the seat.

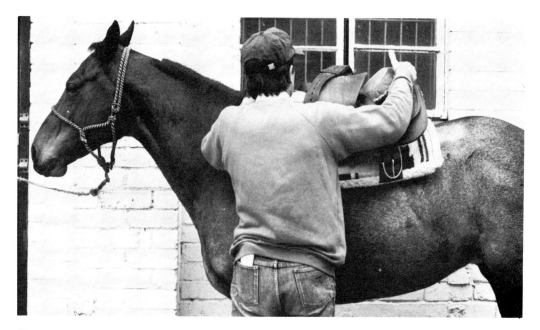

Fig 33 Place the saddle gently on the pad.

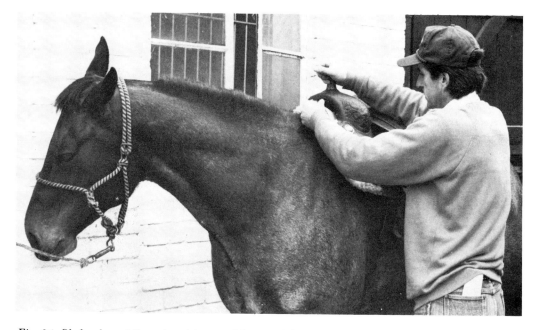

Fig 34 Shake the saddle and pad into position and lift the pad up into the gullet.

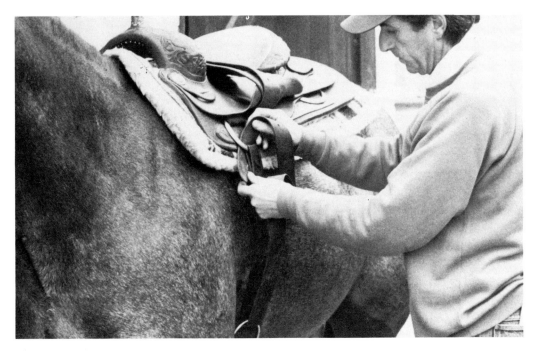

Fig 35 Pass the long latigo through the saddle D-ring.

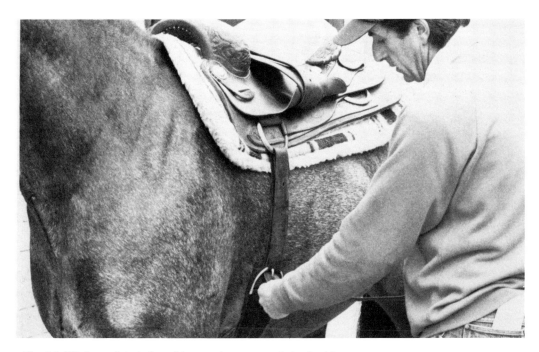

Fig 36 Tighten the girth and insert the tongue of the buckle
into the long latigo.

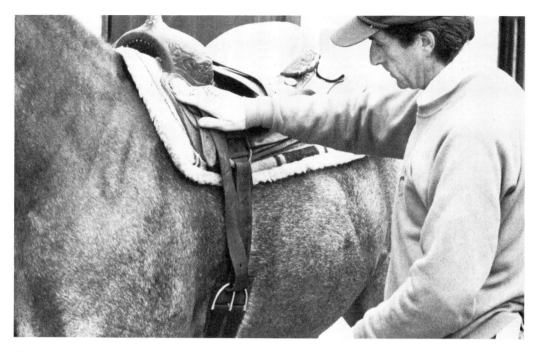

Fig 37 *Insert the remainder of the latigo into the latigo carrier.*

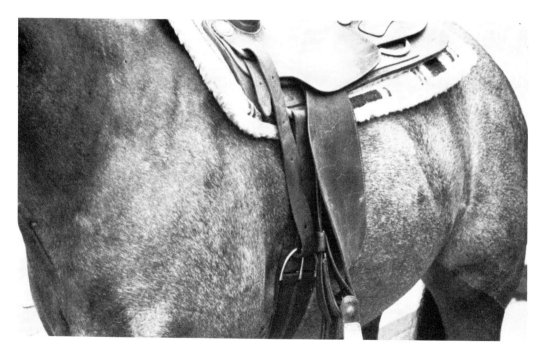

Fig 38 *The horse is now ready for mounting – everything is neat and tidy.*

simply hold the horn and throw it on one-handed, like they do in the western movies, or you will both frighten and hurt your horse and your saddle will probably end up getting damaged too.

Make sure that there is approximately one to two inches (3–5cm) of saddle pad showing at the leading edge of the saddle skirt. Then place your hand on the horn and gently rock the saddle so that both the saddle and pad move into a natural position on the horse's back. With the saddle in place, you should lift it slightly by the horn and draw up the pad and blanket into the gullet. You will then be sure that the saddle does not bear directly on the horse's spine.

Western Girths

There are basically two types of Western girth, or cinch. The cinches I prefer are double-tongued, that is, they have a buckle at both ends. The cinch itself should be extended so that it protects the horse's side from the buckle. The cinch

Fig 39 How to tie off a latigo.

then buckles to the short thick leather billet on the offside of the saddle and to the long latigo on the nearside, in the same way as you would buckle a belt. Because of its length, you usually have to pass the latigo around the cinch and saddle rings twice before buckling it securely. (*See* Fig 36.)

Some older Western cinches have a buckle at one end and a ring at the other. This type buckles to the billet on the offside while at the nearside the long latigo is passed through the ring, pulled snug and then tied off, using a necktie knot, to lie flat under the fender. In both cases, the excess latigo is threaded up through the latigo carrier to hang out of harm's way.

If your saddle has two cinches, I recommend that you remove the rear one as it is not needed for most types of riding. Traditionalists still use them, however, as do calf ropers. When a rear cinch is used, it is important to remember that it must be connected to the front cinch and it must be loose enough so that the horse can expand fully without feeling it, but not so loose that the horse could trap a foot if it lifts it to scratch. If fitted, a rear cinch should be the last thing you do up and the first thing you untie.

Bridles

Western bridles come in four different styles: split-eared, slip-eared, one-eared and brow-band. The first three are all variations on a theme, the horse having only one ear through the bridle. These bridles are convenient and easy to use, and show off a horse that is so good and responsive that you do not need a throat-latch or a nose cavesson.

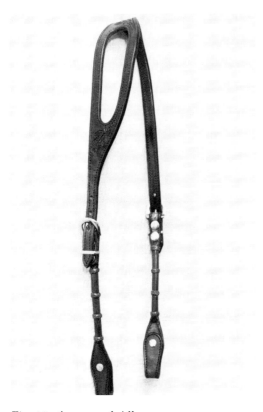

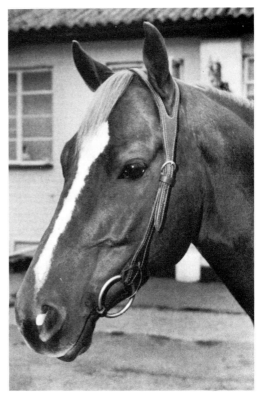

Fig 40 A one-ear bridle.

Fig 41 One-ear bridle on a horse.

Young or unpredictable horses are trained in a conventional brow-band bridle with throatlatch. This is because it is quite possible for an untrained horse to throw its head about and slip off a one-ear or slip-ear bridle, leaving the rider in a very lonely place indeed.

Any Western bridle of whatever design should be made of good quality leather, free from cracks and blemishes. It should fit well, look tidy and enhance your horse's head. The Western horse should look as light as possible. So, ideally, the bridle should be as simple as possible, and made of light leather, preferably the same colour as your saddle and other fittings.

Bitless Bridles

After the restraint of a simple head collar, the first means of control I apply to a young horse in its training is the bosal. The bosal is based on the original Spanish hackamore and is basically a braided rawhide noseband which tapers to a large heel knot. This is attached to a conventional headstall, and plaited horsehair reins, or *mecate*, are attached around the knot.

I prefer the bosal to the more widely used modern mechanical hackamore, as I regard the mechanical hackamore as far too severe to be useful at any stage of the training programme. The simple rawhide bosal, preferably with a rawhide core, can be shaped to fit comfortably around the

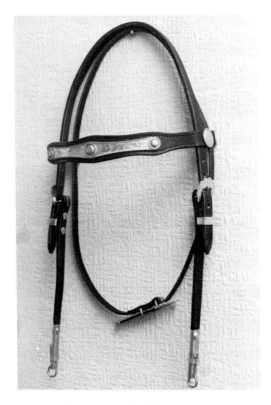

Fig 42 A brow-band bridle.

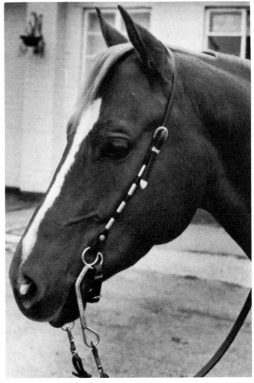

Fig 43 One-eared rolled bridle with fixed cheek curb bit.

horse's nose. It works by applying nose, jaw and poll pressure. At no time, however, does it apply the bone-crunching nutcracker action of the mechanical hackamore.

Another bitless bridle is the side pull. This is a more recent innovation and is simply a waxed rope noseband which allows direct-pull reins to be attached on either side. When using the bosal, because the reins come from the central knot, underneath the jaw, you have to take a wide leading rein to make any directional changes clear to the horse. With the side pull, you can ask for a little direct flexion of the horse's head and neck much more easily.

Traditionalists still prefer to use the bosal, but both these training aids share one common benefit. They enable you to teach a horse all the basics before you ever use a bit and start pulling on its mouth. This helps to produce a lighter and softer horse which is extremely responsive to any rein aids. Furthermore, if at any time later on your horse develops any mouth problems, you will be able to switch back to either of these bridles and continue to ride.

Fig 44 Bosal and mecate.

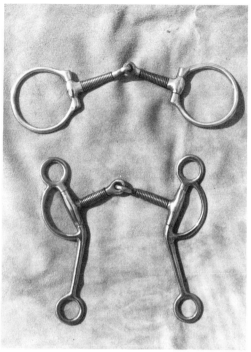

Fig 45 Top: copper-wrapped snaffle bit for horses with dry mouths. Bottom: copper-wrapped shank snaffle.

The Snaffle Bit

After a young horse has completed its training in the bosal or side pull, I will introduce it to an ordinary snaffle bit. This may be a D-ring, O-ring or eggbutt – whichever suits the horse best. The snaffle bit works on the corners of the horse's mouth and has a direct pull ratio of one to one. That means if you put ten pounds (5 kg) of pressure on the reins, you will apply ten pounds (5 kg) of pressure to the horse's mouth. This reduces the chance of you accidentally trying to overpower a difficult horse with the bit.

You should introduce your horse to the bit quite casually so that it does not become frightened by it. Let the horse stand in its stall and carefully slip the bit into place. Watch the horse to make sure that it is not frightened, but otherwise leave it alone for a while to become used to having this strange piece of metal in its mouth. Perhaps even let the horse eat with the bit in place, so that it realises that there really is nothing to be frightened of. I prefer sweet iron snaffles with copper inlays to stainless steel. Horses seem to prefer their taste and so take to them more readily. Only when your horse is working quietly and competently in the snaffle, and can stop, rein back, turn left and right and move up and down smoothly through its paces, should you consider switching to a curb bit.

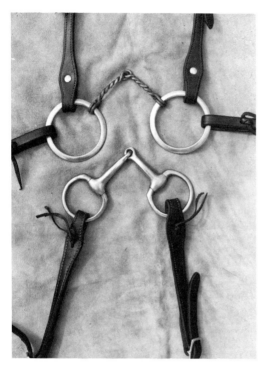

Fig 46 Top: twisted wire snaffle bit, to be used only by experienced riders. Bottom: standard eggbutt snaffle.

The Curb Bit

The curb bit is probably the single most misunderstood piece of Western tack. It is true that curb bits look severe, and in the wrong hands they undoubtedly can be. It is vital to understand, however, that they are not used to restrain a wayward horse but to lighten a perfectly obedient one. Part of the reason for this misconception can be traced to the practice of many English riders who switch from the jointed snaffle to a more severe bit only when they encounter difficulty in controlling their horses. To improve their brakes, they tie the horse's mouth shut and fit whatever bit will stop the horse

when they tug on the reins. Consequently, when they see a curb bit they regard it as an instrument of compulsion rather than a means of lightening the contact required.

To understand how misguided this view is, you have only to watch a finished Western horse working cattle, or performing a reining pattern. No animal will really excel at something it does grudgingly. To perform willingly it must enjoy its work, and this is the approach all good trainers adopt with their horses.

Young horses are first trained in the bosal and then in the snaffle. They are kept in this bit until they reach a standard that most riders would consider completely trained. But the 'finished' Western horse must work even lighter and softer, and so it is taken a step further and introduced to the curb bit. It would be naive to assume, however, that a horse which will not perform a sliding stop in the bosal or snaffle, can be forced to do so with a curb bit. If a horse is to work correctly in the curb, it must already be fully trained and responsive. This point is further confirmed in Western competition classes where finished horses are not allowed to wear a noseband. A horse which is not properly trained, or is being abused by its rider will immediately open its mouth to escape the bit pressure, reducing both the rider's score and the trainer's credibility.

It cannot be overemphasised how important it is that your horse should be trained in stages and never over-bitted. So many riders seem to think that they should buy a curb bit at the same time as they buy their first Western saddle. In fact, it is probably the last thing they will ever need to buy. Whenever I am asked which bit I recommend for schooling or

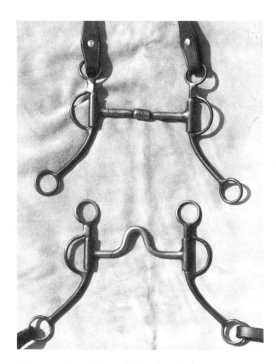

*Fig 47 Greg Darnell handmade bits.
Top: Billy Allen. Bottom: high port.
You can just see the inlaid copper in the
steel mouthpiece.*

The height and width of the port and the length of the shanks directly affect the amount of pressure applied to the horse's mouth. If you have a bit with quite a wide port, then it will apply maximum pressure to the bars of the horse's mouth. I prefer loose-cheeked bits, so that if I am 'forced' to go to a direct rein, the bit will not twist or tilt in the horse's mouth. A direct rein may be called for to correct a horse that is going incorrectly while being reined one-handed. With a loose-cheeked bit I can quietly take the reins in both hands to guide the horse and correct it.

From the snaffle bit, the first curb bit I use is the shanked snaffle, also known as the Billy Allen snaffle. This bit has a jointed mouthpiece with a little copper roller in the centre. This not only acts as a pacifier but also restricts the nutcracker action of the snaffle. Because it is a relatively mild bit, it is an ideal way of introducing the horse to the new experience of the pressure of the curb. If the horse is going well in the shanked snaffle and I want to lighten it still further, I may then introduce a medium or high port curb, depending on the horse.

The spade and half-breed bits should really be considered specialised bits, for advanced riders only. You really need a great deal of understanding of bits and bitting before contemplating their use. Very few riders anywhere in the world use them today. In the past, when they were more widely used, the riders would show off just how light their horses had become by tying a few strands of horse hair between the bit and the reins. To perform all the manoeuvres of Western riding without breaking the hair was proof indeed of a finished horse. Today that test might perhaps be applied in reverse. Only when you can ride that

reschooling a horse, I always answer the bit the horse already readily accepts and goes well in. You should never go on to a curb bit until your horse can do everything you want it to in a simple snaffle.

Choosing a Curb Bit

Curb bits come in a variety of designs, from the jointed, commonly called a shank snaffle, right through to high port bits, and must be chosen and matched carefully to your horse. I like to use handmade curb bits on my finished horses. And, as with my snaffle bits, I prefer curb bits which are made of sweet iron and not stainless steel.

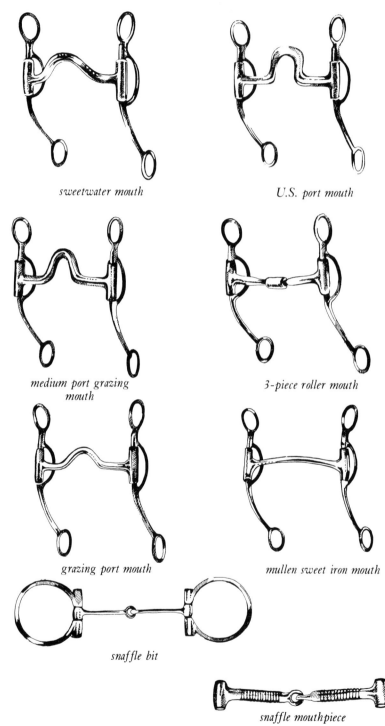

sweetwater mouth

U.S. port mouth

medium port grazing mouth

3-piece roller mouth

grazing port mouth

mullen sweet iron mouth

snaffle bit

snaffle mouthpiece

Fig 48 Western bits and parts of bits.

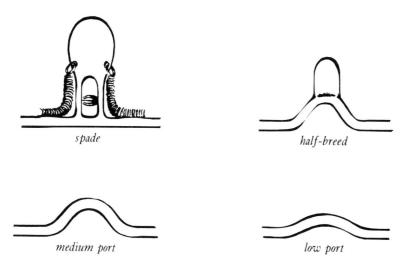

spade

half-breed

medium port

low port

Fig 49 Bit ports and spades.

lightly in a simpler bit should you consider using any of the more severe curb bits.

Reins

There are two basic types of rein, the closed rein known as the Californian closed rein, or romal, and the split or Texas reins. The romal rein was traditionally used by Californian riders and was inherited from the Spanish *conquistadores*. It is essentially a joined rein, rather like conventional English reins, but at the centre a further length of leather, called the romal or popper, is attached, which can be used as a whip or quirt.

The romal rein is held with the reins coming through the bottom of the reining hand and out at the top, with your fingers closed completely around it. The quirt should pass across your body and be held in your other hand, which should rest softly on your thigh. The split, or Texas, reins are simply two lengths of leather, approximately six to seven and a half feet (2–2.5m) long, each attached at one end to the bridle. The split reins are carried with the reins entering the top of the reining hand between the thumb and second finger, with your forefinger placed between them. The remainder of the reins should come out of the bottom of your hand and be allowed to hang down on the same side as the reining hand.

Whichever reins are used, the rein hand should be carried just in front of the saddle horn and above the horse's mane. Your hand should not move more than a few inches either way. You should maintain a light and even contact with the reins, so that you never have to move your rein hand far to apply an aid.

Often, when you see some of the finished Pleasure Class horses, you will see that they have what appears to be an excessive amount of slack in the reins. It is likely, however, that the reins are made of leather at least a quarter of an inch (6mm) thick and two-thirds of an inch (15mm) wide, so their weight, even when slack, gives a contact and even a slight move-

Fig 50 Side-pull reins.

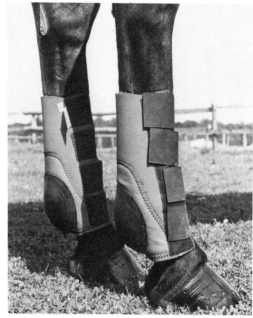

Fig 51 Skid boots, used to protect the fetlocks in sliding stops.

ment of the rein hand provides the horse with any cue it needs.

When training, I prefer to use split reins which I cross over and carry in both hands. When riding two handed, your hands should be four to six inches (10–15cm) apart and you should keep your arm and wrist relaxed. As when riding English style, there should be a straight line from your elbow through your wrist to the bit. I like to see the back of the hand making a straight line with the forearm; that way you will not twist your arm, which can create stiffness and thereby limit your feel.

Boots and Shoes

Whenever you are training your horse you should always kit it out in splint boots, particularly on the front legs which may get knocked during turns and

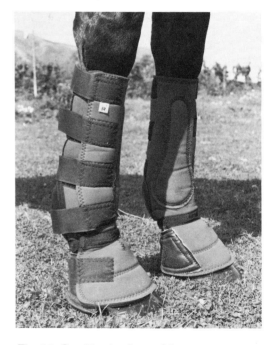

Fig 52 Combination boots: Neoprene padded splint and bell over-reach boot.

Fig 53 Sliding plates to aid sliding stops. These were specially made for us by our farrier, Sam, who copied a sample shoe we obtained from a top American farrier. Note the length, designed to protect the bulbs, and that the outer edge (on left side) is turned upwards to avoid drag on horses that toe out slightly.

spins. Over-reach boots can also be useful. When you start training your horse to rein, you will also require a set of skid boots for the rear legs, to protect the fetlocks from friction burns.

To slide properly, your horse must also be shod with sliding plates at the rear. These are smooth, flat shoes up to one inch (2.5cm) wide which should protrude beyond the heel by a small amount. It is important to note that a horse shod in this way must be ridden carefully on roads or other hard slippery surfaces.

Protective equipment is essential so that your horse does not suffer any pain from minor knocks or kicks it may receive during training. If your horse hurts itself while performing a manoeuvre, it will not stay relaxed and happy, and may even resist when asked to perform the same task again.

6 Basic Training

I have always felt that learning to ride is something of a chicken and egg situation. To ride well both you and your horse need to master many skills and establish a mutual understanding, so that when you ask for a particular response, your horse will comprehend and give it willingly. Similarly, when your horse moves in a particular way, you must sense it and adjust your position and aids accordingly.

In an attempt to sidestep this conundrum and achieve an ideal state of understanding between horse and rider, I like to teach 'riding' and 'schooling' as complementary activities rather than totally separate disciplines. It is my view that in order to ride well it is essential that you learn how to work the horse correctly with tact and feel. You should understand how your horse moves naturally so that when you are on its back you can always work with it and not against it.

Your whole training programme should be founded on the guiding principle of always making it easy for your horse to do what you want it to do, and difficult for it to disobey. If you take this approach to its logical conclusion, your horse will virtually train itself. What is more, the need for punishment or reprimand will be greatly reduced so that your horse will stay happier and certainly more relaxed.

Remember, also, that you cannot train a horse that is either frightened or confused. So you must always keep your horse quiet and calm and never ask it to do something that it finds too difficult, mentally or physically. This last point is another that I will repeatedly stress. It may be unfashionable to liken animals to humans, but I believe that such comparisons do have their uses. Just as you would not ask someone who is totally unfit to attempt a gymnastics exercise or the 100m hurdles, so you should never ask a horse to tackle something it is not yet fit for.

Many times I have seen inexperienced riders beat their horse for failing to jump a small fence, when it has been abundantly clear to all but the rider that the horse was not being stupid or disobedient. The horse refused simply because it was unfit or untrained to do the job easily. It should be clear at once that the guiding principles of our training programme are equally applicable and useful to riders participating in all forms of equestrianism. Perhaps that should not be so surprising, though, as, to rephrase the old saw, 'Times may change, but people and horses don't'.

Getting to Grips with Groundwork

You should by now have assessed your horse's suitability as a Western riding horse, and acquainted yourself with the most important elements of Western tack and clothing. Next, you might reasonably expect that a book about riding would proceed without delay to give you a leg up into the saddle and send you out onto the range.

As I have already said, however, riding is something of a chicken and egg situation. So while most riding manuals might now proceed to discuss the rider's position and the correct aids, I would prefer you to consider whether your horse is sufficiently schooled and well-mannered to be both safe to mount and willing to accept the basic aids once you are on its back.

I believe that if you begin with a little groundwork, your horse will be a lot easier to handle when you come to mount up. I see nothing macho about riding an unschooled horse and I do not enjoy rodeos. If riding is to be pleasurable for horse and rider, it is vital that there is a degree of understanding between both participants. The basis of this understanding is most effectively and safely achieved with all your six feet firmly on the ground. So, here I will explain the basics that we expect our horse to have mastered before we mount. This applies equally well to a young horse freshly backed, as to an older horse which is being retrained as a Western pleasure horse.

First and foremost, you should train your horse to stand square on the ground without a saddle. The horse should have enough confidence in you, the handler, that whenever you halt it, it stands with all four legs square. It should be able to do this before anything else, and will soon come to learn that this quiet, relaxed, square halt is its breathing space, a position it will look forward to adopting after any work that it does. At first you will probably have to nudge the horse or lift a leg or two into the correct position. For this reason you should always accustom your horse to being touched on the legs as well as on the back and under the belly. Do this by first stroking the horse gently in places it enjoys, such as around the eyes, the back of the poll, the neck and withers. In other words, in all the places where horses pet each other.

When you can see by its breathing that it is perfectly relaxed, rub your hands down its back, over its rump and down its shoulders. This is something that horses naturally enjoy and it is a vital part of establishing your bond with your horse. The more you watch your horse interact with other horses, the more you can learn about how you should behave towards it. So often you see people scratching a horse under its chin as if it were a cat. Just as young children hate this treatment, so, too, do horses. The other thing you should do is train your horse to follow you. You can teach this over a period of time whenever you are leading it. Begin by walking a few paces ahead of it and then turn your back to it. Ask it to move forward with a few soft words and perhaps a gentle tug on the lead rope.

Throughout all your training programme you must always avoid conflict. So if your horse will not move forward at first, resist the impulse simply to tug harder on the lead rope. Not only have you no chance of winning any contest of strength, but you will upset your horse and so make it less receptive to what you are trying to teach. You also run the risk of breaking down the relationship of trust which you are trying to build up. So remain patient, and continue asking your horse to walk forward. When it finally does, say 'whoa', and then turn to face it and so help it to stop. Give it time to relax, then adjust all four legs quietly until the horse is standing square.

If you repeat this process over and over, the result will be that when you stand by its side and walk forward, your horse will walk with you. The moment you say 'whoa' and turn and face it, it will stop and stand square, knowing that it can then relax for a moment.

Training should always be fun; even at this simple level it can be taken to quite an exciting stage where your horse will do all this without a lead rein. Yet this simple exercise, once mastered, will make your horse much easier and safer to handle, whether you are leading it from a field to a stable or along a road. More importantly, you will have taken the first important steps along the road of establishing a special bond of trust between you and your horse.

Working Away From Pressure

The next lesson your horse must learn is to move away from pressure. You can teach this by placing your hand against the horse's side in such a way that as you press against it it can turn on the forehand. Later on, when you ride it, it will then understand better what you are trying to achieve as you use your legs to move it around. When you first try to move your horse by hand, if it takes even half a step, release the pressure instantly. Then praise it, pet it and let it relax. If you rush these basics, you can spoil a horse forever. Work slowly, day by day and always remain calm, firm and insistent. You should then never need to punish a horse for doing wrong. Almost all horses want to please, but they can only respond correctly if they understand what you want them to do.

While working your horse from the ground you can also start to teach it to flex its neck. Do this by turning its head one way and then the other, slowly and softly, holding the head collar, sidepull or bosal. Watch to see whether the horse will give its nose to the rein hand nice and smoothly, without moving its shoulders or hindquarters. If you repeat this exercise every day, asking for a little more flexion each time, you will slowly increase your horse's suppleness. This will make many of the riding exercises you will do later much easier for the horse to perform.

Once your horse understands that it must move away from pressure, you can teach it the turn on the haunches by standing at its shoulder and gently pushing its shoulder with one hand while leading its nose in the desired direction with the other. It may be a little rough at first, but do not try to overpower the horse if it is not yet ready to tackle this manoeuvre. As a trainer, your best tool is patience and your most valuable skill is the sensitivity to tailor the training programme to match your horse's ability to learn.

Once your horse leads nicely and will follow you, you can develop this bond of trust by introducing it to obstacles on the ground. You can encourage it to pick up its feet over poles, to stand quietly beside gates and even to consider reining back. This important manoeuvre must, however, be approached very carefully and with gentle persuasion.

Beginning the Rein Back

To teach the rein back, apply a little gentle backwards pressure with the head

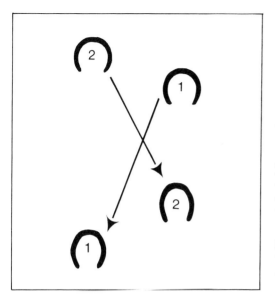

Fig 54 The sequence of the legs during a rein back.

collar. Reinforce it with a little hand pressure on the horse's chest and say the word 'back'. As soon as you sense that your horse is about to move, relax your hands. The first time the horse takes just one step backwards you should praise it and let it relax and stand up square. The moment it lifts its front leg off the ground to take a step back, you know it is going to complete the stride. So, by releasing the pressure as quickly as you can, you teach the horse to look forward to completing the step. (*See* Fig 76.)

Avoiding Problems

Many novice trainers run into difficulties as soon as they attempt an exercise, such as the rein back, that their horse seems unable or unwilling to learn. At first sight you appear to be in a no-win situation. If you abandon the lesson, the horse will have learnt how to evade work. If, on the other hand, you persist, you may end up in a battle which will damage the trust between you and your horse. It is always easy to be wise after an event, however; the key to successful training is to be wise before the event! Training is a step-by-step process. It is vital that you are constantly aware of how quickly your horse is learning and never progress to step two until step one has been mastered thoroughly.

When praising your horse, stay quiet and soft in both voice and hand. Provided you accept the half-step backward or the tiniest turn on the forehand with praise, your horse will learn willingly and you will never end up in a fight. It is worth remembering that few horses are genuinely bad tempered or ill natured at birth. So, whenever your horse resists something, try to understand why. Perhaps something has frightened it. A frightened or nervous horse cannot be trained, so first try to relax it. On the other hand, it may be that your instrucions were not clear enough and your horse has become confused.

Think back to how you felt at school when a teacher asked you something you did not understand, and imagine the problems facing a horse. Whenever you feel that your horse has become confused, it is a good idea to return to something easy that you know your horse can already do. Then, later, when its confidence has been restored, return to the lesson in hand, concentrating on making your wishes as clear as possible.

The experts tell us that the horse has the mind of a three-year-old child. If that is true, then you must learn to think like a teacher in kindergarten. Teaching is

Fig 55 *The traditional method of mounting – facing the rear of the horse.*

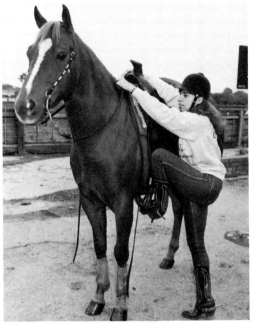

Fig 56 *The usual position for mounting, with the rider facing the horse's head.*

problem-solving in reverse. Limit the possible solutions to the only correct one and the lesson is learnt. If a horse will not rein back correctly, lead it to the corner of your arena or field. Keep it calm and quiet and ask it to go back. Faced with barriers to left and right, it will choose the easiest route and take a step backwards. Once it has readily taken one step, ask for two and so on. Soon the horse will rein back, perfectly straight, anywhere.

Only when you have taught your horse to follow you, stop on command, stand square, turn on the forehand, turn on the haunches and rein back, with you on the ground beside it, should you consider tacking up and mounting.

Mounting

Mounting the Western horse can be done in two ways. The traditional way is to begin by facing the rear of the horse. The more commonly used method, however, is to stand at a slight angle to the horse, facing the front. You should gather up the reins and hold them so as not to allow the horse to go forward. You then place your right hand on the swell or saddle horn, and your left foot in the stirrup.

If you have done your basic training thoroughly, your horse will not even consider moving forward. You can then spring from the floor into an upright position and quietly lift your leg over the back of the horse and very gently allow yourself to sink into the saddle. If you spring up roughly, throw your leg over, kicking the horse's hindquarters in the process, and then slam down in the

Fig 57 Swinging a leg over the horse.

Fig 58 Mounted and ready to walk on.

saddle, you will cause a great deal of discomfort to your horse. It will then quickly learn to associate this unpleasant experience with having someone on its back and dread being ridden. Worse still, it may even try to escape by moving off. This will then force you to grab the reins to stop it. So, before you even begin your ride you are in a rein-tugging conflict with your horse.

Having mounted correctly, it is a good idea to sit quietly for a couple of minutes, with the horse standing square, before moving off. This will encourage the horse to relax and stay quiet and not become overexcited by the prospect of a ride out. Moreover, it is an excellent opportunity for you to collect your thoughts and concentrate on the task in hand.

What makes riding such a truly involving and enjoyable activity is the combination of two living creatures achieving things neither can do on its own. Yet it is all too easy, in this hectic, mechanical world, simply to jump on a horse and expect it to perform like a machine. To ride well you must have an empathy with your horse, and a minute or two's quiet concentration before setting off is the ideal way to forget all your troubles and tune in to your horse.

The Basic Position

Whenever I mount my horse, I like to stand up in the stirrups and allow my heels to drop down. I then bend my knees until my crotch touches the saddle and rotate my pelvis until I am sitting on my seatbones. If you follow this simple procedure each time before you ride off, you should find yourself in exactly the right position, sitting upright with your shoulders, hips and heels in line.

Another useful exercise is to stand in the stirrups with your heels down and knees slightly bent. For novices this soon teaches the lesson that the best way to maintain your balance is to let the weight flow down into the heels. It is also an ideal exercise for strengthening the legs. Strong legs are vital for effective and subtle leg aids. Regular practice in keeping the knees bent will also make you better able to absorb shocks through the ankles and knees while at the same time keeping them free and relaxed.

Moving Off

When you are comfortable, gather up the reins and take up a light contact on the horse's mouth. This light contact should be taken *after* the horse has flexed at the poll. You do not want your horse to move off in a slovenly manner with its nose poking out the front door. You should then ask it to 'walk on' as you relax the reins slightly and close your legs around it.

I like to use a lot of voice control when training, as it allows me to keep the physical aids that much lighter. Ideally, your horse should move off in a straight line, but forward movement is more important than direction in the early stages. If you have done your groundwork properly, your horse should know it must move away from pressure. So if your horse is not moving straight, then you should be able to correct it to the left or right with your legs.

You must also learn to influence your horse by your position and seat. To do this you must become flexible in the

lower back and pelvis so that you can move with your horse and absorb the concussion of its legs hitting the ground. Your aim should be to stay in the middle of the saddle in an upright, relaxed manner, and allow your pelvis to move in time with the horse. In a short space of time you will be able to influence the speed of your horse simply by increasing or decreasing the pace or length of your pelvic movement. Your ultimate goal is to be able to influence your horse's pace without the need to drive it with your legs. You want to teach your horse that a leg aid is something to move away from, not something that merely means move forward at ever-increasing speed.

Another experiment to carry out at this stage, is to place extra weight in one or other stirrup. You should find that the horse will then move to one side, seeking out your weight. It is a bit like balancing a ruler on your finger, if the ruler falls away from you to one side, you must move the finger underneath it to balance it again. When doing this exercise, however, you must not lean to the side with your shoulders. When I talk about weight transference, I am talking about a minimal hip movement – just the subtle weighting of one seatbone or the other.

As I said in the introduction, riding and schooling are complementary skills. Both demand sensitivity. Whenever someone gets on a horse for the first time, they always ask how they can make it go, turn and stop. Armed with a few simple instructions they then believe they can ride. Unfortunately, many riders never seem to progress beyond this simplistic view. To ride well, however, you must spend every moment you can in the saddle, feeling how the horse moves under you and how it responds to your every movement. That way you will soon realise that there is no such thing as a simple aid, and you will begin to understand how your horse really responds to your various movements and transferences of weight.

Because you have taught your horse to flex its head, you can use the reins to enhance your leg aids. Let the horse walk forward in a relaxed manner, and then lead it one way and then another with the reins and see what response you get. If you achieve even the slightest success with a particular aid, then release your horse and praise it. It is important to spend a lot of time at the walk and not progress hastily to faster gaits. The walk is a passive gait and ideal for training. The trot is also a calm gait, but do not be too keen to work up to the canter. For the horse this is an escape gait, indelibly associated with fear and flight.

Teach your horse everything first at the walk, then at the trot and last at the canter. The training at each gait will give the horse time to understand what is required of it, as well as the time to become fit and supple enough to undertake the next stage of training. If at any time your horse finds difficulty in learning something at a faster gait, repeat the exercise at a slower gait.

When riding in straight lines or circles, it is a useful exercise to try to visualise the line you are on. If you imagine yourself straddling this line, then whenever you stray off to one side, you should instinctively use your legs to get back on course, and not your hands. Yanking on the reins to correct a change in direction will merely set up a fishtailing movement and will not get you smoothly back on course.

This visualisation will also help you to learn to detect whether your horse is out of line because a shoulder is dropping, the barrel is twisted, the hip is tipped or the head and neck are out of position. Whatever type of riding you do, your performance will be enhanced as you improve your feel. The quicker you learn to detect when something is going wrong and remedy it, the better your horsemanship will become.

Reschooling Your Horse to Western

By far the majority of riders turning to Western riding already have horses which have been schooled and ridden in the English style. For these riders, reschooling their horses is the obvious answer. Provided it has a suitable conformation and temperament, there is no reason why any horse cannot be retrained and ridden Western.

As far as serious competition is concerned, greatest success will usually be achieved on horses trained exclusively in the Western disciplines. It is still possible, however, to enjoy the softness and quietness of the Western style, the comfort of the Western saddle and the challenge of Western competitions on an older horse already trained in other disciplines.

In most cases you would not need to follow the whole training programme as laid out for the young horse; however, there is no harm in going back to basics. You might like to consider at this stage whether your horse leads easily, stops on command, stands square and moves away from leg pressure, as these are the foundations upon which much of Western riding is built.

I would certainly recommend that you

75

take your horse through the same process of free schooling in the roundpen (*see* page 79), particularly if your horse has not been schooled in any way for some time. Such work will teach the horse to listen to you and will help to reinforce the bond between you. The chances are that if you have had your horse for any length of time, you will have come to take each other for granted. When reschooling, however, both you and your horse must make more effort and work harder together. Your horse must also be encouraged to work in different ways, something which, being a creature of habit, it may not find easy at first.

So begin slowly. Although you know, and your horse knows, how to trot, canter and turn, pretend that you do not. Begin your reschooling entirely at the walk before increasing pace. One of the hardest lessons your horse might have to learn is to relax and work quietly. A good Western horse should not throw fits or challenge your control. You may also have to work on improving your horse's collection. If so, concentrate on manoeuvres such as the rollback, for nothing encourages engagement as much as this turn over the haunches.

Always try to make the schooling a pleasant and enjoyable experience for your horse. That way any bad experiences the horse may have had in the past, or bad habits it may have acquired more recently, can be worked over and, in most cases, eliminated.

To reschool an older horse, you often need to be even more perceptive than when working with a young, green horse. While a young horse will show obvious signs of confusion, fear or exhaustion, the older horse can more easily dupe you. It is very easy to rush an older horse that appears to know what is wanted of it. So take things steady. If your horse has a fault, whether it is head shaking or running into canter, do not accept it. Get back to basics and try to find its cause. Remember that faults become habits and habits become faults.

Most problems in older horses can be traced to stiffness. Everyone wants an athletic horse, but it takes time and work to make a horse an athlete. So make the effort to see if your horse has any stiffness, and if it does, work on making it supple. More often than not that will cure the problem for good. You should also make sure that your horse will move away easily from leg pressure. If you observe horses in a field, you will see that most of them, especially the dominant ones, do not yield to pressure, but push or kick against it! So you must overcome this natural reaction and teach your horse to move away from pressure. Again, it might be best to go right back to the beginning and work your horse from the ground. Start by pushing it gently with your hand, and when it moves away, release the pressure and praise it.

The older horse will almost certainly also benefit from schooling with Bowling reins. Even if your horse has quite a hard mouth, you should find that by teaching it to find its own level, and escape rein pressure by flexing at the poll, eventually you will actually restore its mouth and lighten it. In extreme cases you could even try your horse in the bosal. Normally, however, I would school most older horses in a snaffle bit.

Once you feel that your horse can comfortably manage all the basics and, above all, that it has adopted a suitably receptive attitude to this new programme, then you can take it out into an arena or field to work. From then on you should follow the same basic programme as for the younger horse, only perhaps being a little more selective and working harder on the manoeuvres it finds most difficult.

Although, theoretically, you can work an older, fitter horse longer and harder than a young one, remember that horses, just like people, learn best in short intensive bursts of training. So keep your schooling lessons reasonably short. You can always reward your horse with a hack out afterwards and put some of your schooling into practice as you go.

7 Training the Young Horse

It is difficult to be precise about the age at which you should begin training your horse in earnest. Age in years is actually less important here than the horse's build, conformation and mentality. A well-put-together American Quarter horse with a good mind can usually be introduced to training at the age of two. However, this breed does seem to mature earlier than others and two years old would be far too young in many cases.

It is up to you to assess the development of your own horse. By all means make an early start on a well-built, sensible youngster. If at any time you feel that it is becoming stressed, however, back off and let it out to play. I cannot overemphasise the importance of making the training programme an enjoyable exercise for the young horse. Some two-year-olds can even be backed and ridden before being turned away until they are three, when their serious training begins. It is my experience that when horses can be trained in this way they stay sound and strong and are mentally stable by the end of the third year.

With Appaloosas, Palominos, cobs and Thoroughbred crosses, I use basically the same technique while remaining aware that youngsters of these breeds do take a little longer to mature. You must always remember that much of what you do with a young horse at this stage of its training will have lasting effect. So if at any time you find yourself in a situation with which you cannot cope, it is vital that you seek help from a professional trainer.

Most good horse trainers will willingly listen and give advice. Rather than spoil a good horse, it may even be best that you should swallow your pride and send your horse to a trainer for a while so that the foundations can be properly established. Bear in mind, though, that it generally takes a minimum of three months for a good trainer to establish a rapport with a horse and lay down a good foundation for future development.

The Round Pen

All the young horses I train are started off in a round pen. This is an absolutely invaluable schooling aid which can be constructed easily by anyone. It takes up relatively little space and need not be expensive, but, within it, all the fundamental schooling of your horse can be accomplished easily and in great safety. The typical round pen is simply a circular arena, ideally about forty-five feet (15m) in diameter. The sides should be about six feet (2m) high and boxed in. For the first yard or so you should line the pen with thick kicking boards. On my pen I have also covered these with rubber, taken from old three-feet-wide (1m) conveyor belts. The footing should be about four inches (10cm) deep and of a free-draining material such as sea sand, or a proprietary equivalent such as Pasada.

Alternatively, you can make up a temporary round pen, using hurdles or fencing, in any field corner. The advan-

Fig 59 A typical round pen.

tage of a permanent, solid pen, however, is that it is much safer and, being closed in, the horse will concentrate much more on your instruction.

When you first introduce your young horse to the round pen you should do so slowly, perhaps just leading it in, around and out a couple of times before attempting any schooling. If the horse is to learn anything in the pen it must first be calm and relaxed.

Free Schooling

You should already have taught your horse to stand square, to move away from pressure and, above all, to trust and respond to you. Now you can start with some free schooling. To begin with you can run the horse free or in a head collar, but soon you should accustom it to wearing the bosal together with a roller, and splint boots on both front and hind legs.

By standing in the middle of the arena and driving your horse round the outside at walk, trot and canter, you can observe how the horse moves naturally. By keeping the horse out on the rail, you are also training it to put a slight arc in the length of its body while staying upright. At any time when you wish the horse to stop, you should say 'whoa', and cut across the arena to block its path. When it has stopped, you should go to it and make a fuss of it. This way it learns both that it has done well and, just as importantly, to associate you with praise and affection.

Continue this simple exercise at walk and trot, until the horse will stop easily at both gaits. Soon you will find you can bring it smoothly from trot to walk simply by taking a pace forward. The benefit of free schooling is that at no time is anything flapping around the horse's

Fig 60 A 'green' horse at the trot. Free-schooled, the horse turns by bending to the outside with its shoulder falling in.

nose or pulling on it. The horse is simply trusting you and doing what you ask. Every time your horse does something correctly, praise it and let it relax and fill up on air. That way it will learn to relax and enjoy its work. If your horse does not enjoy your training sessions, you will have a tough time teaching it anything.

Remember also not to overtax a young horse. More short lessons are better than fewer long ones. Just as in medicine, prevention is far better and easier than cure, and if you can avoid problems by keeping your horse relaxed and happy, you will find life a lot easier than if you hit trouble and then have to sort out the consequences. Horses are like people in that some are better athletes while others are more intelligent. So, how hard and fast you teach your horse will depend very much on both its conformation and aptitude. As a rule, though, it is always better to do too little than too much.

It is very easy to get carried away while training and lose track of time,

especially when things are going well and you are really enjoying yourself. If you ask for just a little too much, however, your horse may become overtaxed and develop a fault. So be prepared to switch off a little earlier. End with something easy and plenty of praise. That way all your horse's associations with the training process will be favourable.

Beginning the Rollback

After perhaps a week or so of working your horse in the round pen, you can begin to teach it the basis of one of the key Western manoeuvres, the rollback. The rollback is a 180-degree turn over the haunches and allows a quick change of direction at any pace.

Begin this lesson by asking the horse to walk quietly around the rail. When it is walking up well and listening to you, ask it to halt and then move quickly to its head so that it turns away from you

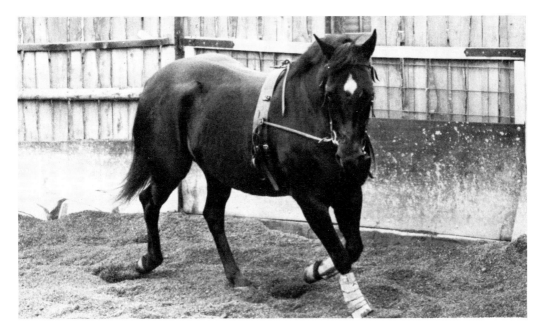

Fig 61 A 'green' horse at the trot. The inside rein causes the neck to flex, making the shoulder rise and the horse become better balanced. Remember, this is its first lesson!

towards the fence. In its efforts to turn quickly it should plant its inside hindleg, and move its front legs around itself. Because it is restricted by the rail, it will shorten its body up and execute a turn on the haunches. When it does this be sure to praise it and then allow it to walk out quietly.

Practise this exercise little and often. The idea is to accustom the horse to turning over its haunches which you must do by making it move away from you. The lesson the horse must learn, however, is the turn, not that you are something it should fear.

Canter Work

When your horse walks and trots nicely on both reins, you can then ask it to canter. Try not to chase it with the lunge whip, but use your voice as much as possible. Cluck and kiss and encourage it with a raised hand to move up from trot to canter. Should the horse strike off on the wrong lead, it will feel very unbalanced. In this event step back quietly and then move to its head so that it breaks gait. As soon as it does, urge it back into canter. When it picks up the correct lead it should feel much more balanced. At first you should simply allow the horse to seek its own level. Do not worry about speed or head carriage. All that is required is that the horse moves forwards and is on the correct lead.

You should be able to shut the horse down at any time by moving towards its head and asking it to trot or walk. As soon as it does so, step back and praise it. Once the horse has become balanced and relaxed again in the new gait, bring it down to the halt and give it time to relax

Fig 62 *At canter the horse shows a greater degree of shoulder drop, thus losing its balance to the inside and scrambling around the turn. If you can imagine a rider on top of this horse, you can see how very dangerous and unstable this way of turning is.*

Fig 63 *By getting the horse to flex to the inside a little, I am beginning to rectify the situation. As training progresses, this will improve greatly as the horse begins to balance itself better, and it will become more upright and in a safer position to ride.*

and fill up on air. Use these moments to walk up to it and reward it and enter its mental bubble.

Patience and care at this time will help you to create the bond of trust you need between you and your horse. The more your horse trusts you now, the easier you will find the next stages of saddling up and backing. Whenever you work with your horse you should make sure that you are relaxed and in the correct frame of mind. For example, it is not a good idea to go out training when you have just had a rude letter from your bank manager!

Ground Driving

After free schooling your horse at the walk, trot and canter, the next stage is to consider ground driving and turns. I like to use the bosal for ground driving, and at the same time I will acquaint the horse with the saddle. When introducing your horse to the saddle, begin first by laying the blanket and pad on its back. If the horse becomes anxious, talk softly and reassure it until it relaxes again. Then place the saddle gently on its back. Keep reassuring it and, once it is calm, do up the girth lightly.

Most young horses will have already had a rug and roller on at some stage, so they should not be frightened by the girth. Cinch it up just enough so that the saddle cannot slip round. Then allow the horse to walk free for a while until it relaxes. Then tie the stirrups together underneath the belly and attach a set of driving reins to the bosal. Run the driving reins through the stirrups and around the back, and allow your horse to get used to them while stationary. When the horse seems to have accepted them,

ask it to walk forward, holding the lines exactly as you would drive any horse.

You can then practise turning left with gentle tugs on the left rein while relaxing the outside rein and turning right by applying the opposite aids. The horse already knows the word 'whoa'. So now, when you require the horse to stop, apply a gentle nose pressure with the reins and say 'whoa' at the same time. The horse will quickly associate the pressure with the word of command. This will have the effect of reinforcing both aids. Once at the halt, praise your horse and let it stand a while and think about what it has just done.

You can now move to the centre of the arena by lengthening the outside rein and shortening the inside one a little. This will allow you to put your horse back out on the rail while you stand in the middle where it can see you. Then, with the horse stopped, you can put a little extra pressure in the outside rein and ask the horse to turn around towards the fence. As it has already learned the rollback during its free schooling, it knows the easiest way to turn. So now you will find that you are able to turn your horse nicely over its haunches with just the lightest aid from the leading rein.

By standing in the middle of the round pen it is quite easy for you to push the horse up into trot and perform the same exercises again, without having to run like mad yourself. The outer perimeter of the round pen means that you do not constantly have to keep guiding the horse in the circle and therefore you can avoid unnecessary rein pressure. Remember, the bosal should be used with gentle tugs; constant contact would soon deaden the feeling in the horse's nose and jaw.

Fig 64 Here I am about to receive a lesson in driving four years
ago from Pete Bowling. Training can be fun!

Fig 65 A study in concentration: driving a three-year-old
gelding. Some three years later, this Quarter Horse achieved
fifth place in Western Riding and Versatility in the European
Championships.

Fig 66 Using driving reins and a bosal in the round pen.

Backing

As soon as you feel that the horse is comfortable about turning left and right in response to the rein pressure, and is totally relaxed at all times, it is time for you to consider backing it. If you have done your basic training correctly, your horse will have total confidence in you and will know that you mean it no harm.

Begin by untying the stirrups. Then take one of the driving reins and loop it around the saddle horn. Now tighten the girth. If the horse is relaxed, send it out on the rail again with only the driving rein attached to the saddle horn. This will allow you to put a little pressure on the saddle by tugging the rein, and so accustom the horse to a little weight and movement in the saddle area.

If the horse bucks or gets frightened you can calm it quickly for you still have your feet safely on the ground! Only when you see that the horse has accepted this new sensation and is calm and quiet, should you consider stepping aboard. This important stage must not be rushed. First remove the driving rein and then, when you have your horse's full attention, ask a helper to stand by the horse's head and pet it. You can then place one foot in the stirrup and slowly put a little weight in it. The Western stirrup is designed for a quick and easy dismount, so you can remove your foot quickly again at the first sign of trouble.

If the horse remains calm, stand up in the stirrup and gently lean over the saddle. All the time you do this you should be talking quietly and stroking the horse to reassure it. Provided you do not rush and your horse has total confidence in you, you should not encounter any problems whatsoever. You should then lift your right leg over the horse's back and very quietly and gently sit down in the saddle, still stroking the horse, praising it and keeping it calm and relaxed.

Once you have sat straight and still in the saddle for a moment, dismount slowly and gently. Repeat the mounting and dismounting several times and from both sides. When I mount a young horse, I will often rub its hindquarters with my right boot as I swing my leg over. This way the horse will be less likely to spook should someone ever mount carelessly and accidentally kick the horse in the process.

If all has gone well, you should now be in the saddle of a calm, quiet horse which has accepted your presence without question. Now you can ask the horse to walk on. You do not do this with your legs, however. Instead, your helper should slowly step forward and encourage the horse to follow. It does not matter if you have to sit and wait for half an hour before you move off, but you must let your horse take the first few steps itself. This is because these first few steps will be rather unsteady as the horse learns to move and balance your weight at the same time.

When it finally does step forward, praise it all the way. After a few paces stop it by saying 'whoa' as your helper turns to stand in front of you. You can repeat this process for a few more steps but then you should dismount, praise your horse and end the lesson. The horse can then be stabled or turned out for the rest of the day for it has done well.

The following day you can continue the lesson by walking a little further. When you want to stop, combine the word 'whoa' with a little extra weight in your heels, round your back up and even apply a little rein pressure. Your horse should now simply repeat the behaviour it learnt on the ground, stopping promptly and standing nice and square. You can even ask it to take one step back by taking up a light rein pressure and momentarily holding it. Usually a horse will then take one or a half pace back, at which point you must instantly release all your aids and praise it.

When you feel that your horse has learnt to balance your weight properly at the walk, you can dispense with your assistant. You can then begin to practise turns, by applying a little rein pressure to turn left and then to turn right. Because your horse has learnt to understand and enjoy your requests when you worked it from the ground, it should respond eagerly.

Start with just the lightest pressure to see what response you get. If the horse moves just one inch in the correct direction, release the pressure and praise it. This may all sound rather long-winded, but I cannot overemphasise the importance of this early basic training. If at any time you rush these early lessons, you are chancing your luck. It is extremely easy to overload a young horse's mind, and if fear and confusion are allowed to creep in, you will not only find the horse impossible to teach today, but you will sow the seeds of disaster for tomorrow.

Given the right type of horse, these training methods will produce a mount that has a desire and a willingness to please. In all my experience of sorting out 'problem' horses, I have found that almost all difficulties can be traced to bad handling or to basic groundwork being rushed or done incorrectly. To rephrase a familiar maxim, 'there are few bad horses, but many bad owners.'

Trotting

Only when your horse is perfectly balanced at the walk, and can turn left and right, stop and rein back a few paces, should you proceed to the trot. You should encourage the horse to trot with your seat, by clucking and asking it to 'trot on', words it should by now have learned from your groundwork. If you need to use any leg pressure, it must be exceedingly light.

Once in trot, just let your horse carry you around the pen at its own speed until it achieves a balanced pace. The round pen really is an invaluable aid here. During the young horse's first few attempts at different paces, it will constantly need to move its head and neck to balance itself. The last thing you want to have to do at this stage is pull its head around with the reins and worry about direction. In the confined space of the round pen, however, the horse will naturally gravitate to the outside rail, allowing you to relax and concentrate on sitting straight and still in the centre of the saddle.

Cantering

Once the trot has been mastered, you can proceed to the canter. Again, you should not worry about speed or direction; if your groundwork has been done correctly the horse should automatically adopt the lead on which it feels most comfortable. So, if you use only the gentlest pressure from your outside leg, your horse should strike off into canter on the correct lead.

If it does pick up the incorrect lead, do not haul it back with the reins. Instead, sit back and wait for it to break gait naturally. As soon as it does, cluck and urge it back into canter once more. The horse will soon realise which lead is more comfortable. Just as children learn something best when they work it out for themselves, wherever possible let your horse do the same.

It all sounds rather simple I know, but that is the basis of effective training. Keep everything simple and your horse will understand what you want. Make the training enjoyable and your horse will work willingly. Remember, horses love to find their own level.

When your horse has learnt and mastered all the basic manoeuvres in the round pen, you can take it to a larger arena and give it some space to work in. When you do, however, begin quietly at the walk and work slowly through the same basic programme.

The Transition to the Snaffle Bit

When your horse has mastered the basics at all the gaits and can turn, stop and rein back in the bosal, it is ready to receive the snaffle bit. You should find that riding with a little more contact in a bit presents no difficulties whatsoever. In fact, more problems come from the rider than the horse at this stage. It is vital that you use the reins lightly and do not exploit the extra power the bit gives you at the expense of the other aids. If you run into any problems, revert to the bosal and remind yourself that the horse can perform without any need for you to haul on the bit.

Fig 67 Note how Keo can flex easily without dropping a shoulder as he gives to the lightest pressure of the left rein.

Fig 68 Sheila has relaxed the left rein and taken up a gentle contact on the right rein; Keo obliges readily and easily.

Head Setting

Once your horse has accepted the bit and will respond to it in a relaxed and easy manner, the time has come to start controlling the way the horse works. Now that it has become accustomed to balancing your weight, you can start thinking about keeping its head where you want it rather than where it wants it. Ideally, your horse should flex at the poll and carry its head at such a height that its eyes are level with its withers. The best way to work towards this goal is to return once again to free schooling in the round pen.

Tack up your horse and then attach the left rein to the left stirrup and the right rein to the right stirrup, so that each rein has a little weight in it. Then ask your horse to walk out on the rail. Each time the horse raises its nose above a certain point, the heavy stirrups will apply a little pressure on the bars of its mouth. To start

with the horse may well react by trying to raise its nose even higher to escape the pressure. Because the weight thus increases, however, and is also reinforced by the stirrups bumping against it lightly, the horse will soon realise that the easiest way to escape the pressure is to drop its nose.

Once the horse accepts this restraint totally, and will work in a completely relaxed way at walk, trot and canter, it is ready to be introduced to what I call the Bowling rein. This is simply a piece of rope with a dog clip on each end. You clip one end to the bit, pass the rope down between the horse's legs, up over the saddle, back between the horse's legs and up to clip onto the other side of the bit.

You must be able to adjust the length of the rein so that it is not too tight. If the horse is to learn the correct head carriage, it must learn that the required position frees it from any pressure so that it learns

Fig 69 *Teaching a horse to flex, by tying its head to one side so that the resistance is only to itself, not us. The rein must not be too tight. The horse must have room to escape the pressure.*

Fig 70 *Tying the reins to the stirrups in preparation for using Bowling rein. This trains the young horse to yield to pressure on the bit. When it flexes at the poll, the stirrups hang naturally, and the horse frees itself from the pressure.*

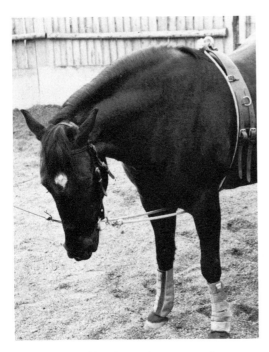

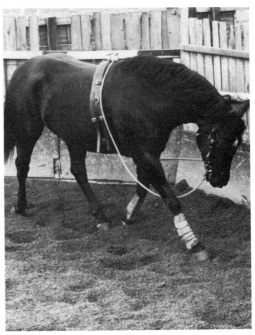

Fig 71 *The Bowling rein must not be made too tight until the horse begins to understand what is required of it. There must be an escape from the pressure if the horse is to learn anything.*

Fig 72 *The same horse, eight days later. Now the horse is relaxed, giving to the bridle; the hindquarters show greater engagement; the shoulder and the ribcage are lifted up.*

to enjoy moving that way. Begin with the reins loose enough so the horse only feels pressure when it raises its head. As soon as it carries its head level and flexes at the poll, it should be able to escape the pressure totally. You will notice, as you ask your horse to walk out, that the movement of its legs causes a minor, very light see-sawing of the bit which reinforces the slight pressure. Your horse will soon find that if it carries its head in a level position, with its poll flexed, it can get away from this pressure.

When the horse first drops its head and neck down a little, it will probably feel slightly unbalanced and on the forehand and so will speed up. This, in turn, will make the horse want to raise its head in order to slow down again, whereupon it

will encounter the rein pressure and the process will be repeated. What usually happens is that after a few minutes the horse will put its head down, round up in the loins, engage its hindquarters and rebalance itself while, at the same time, escaping the pressure of the rein. In effect the horse has taught itself what we want it to do because we have made it easy for it.

Clearly, if your horse is not to be completely spooked by this experience and throw an almighty fit, it is vital that the Bowling rein is not too tight. Do not try to set the head in the perfect position straightaway. School the horse with the rein quite slack to begin with and then shorten it in stages, a little at a time, until the head carriage is spot on. This process must not be rushed and may take from

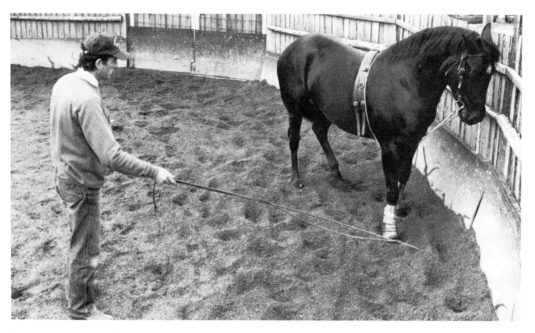

Fig 73 'Shutting the horse down' by stepping across in front of it. I am now about to turn the horse towards the rail; the beginning of training it to engage deeper with its hindquarters.

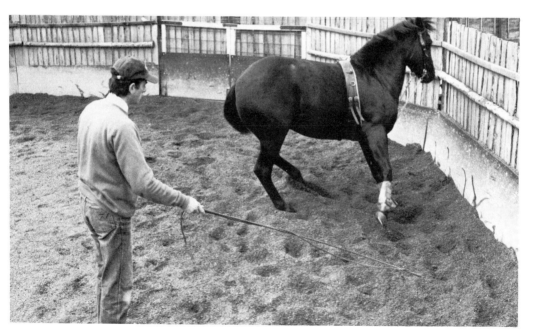

Fig 74 'Pushing' the horse through the turn. The horse learns to engage deeper and move around itself.

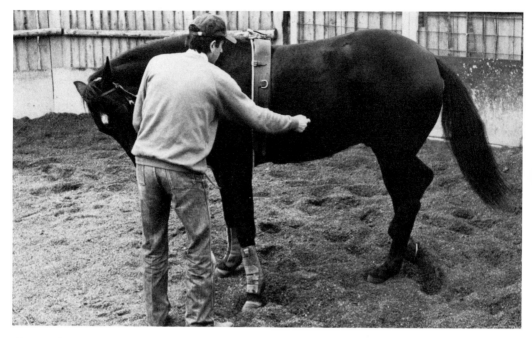

Fig 75 *Initiating the turn on the forehand at an early stage. I am pushing the horse at approximately the place where my leg will be when I am mounted.*

one to two weeks. If at any time the horse appears frightened by the restriction of its head carriage, loosen off the rein and begin again. Your horse must always have a position it can go to that frees it from rein pressure.

As with all schooling, it is better to progress slowly and steadily forward than to rush along taking one step forward and two steps back. The Bowling rein is an extremely useful schooling aid, but if you are in any doubt about how to use it, I would advise you to learn from someone who has already used it successfully. When your horse is working comfortably in the round pen, and has the correct head carriage, you can remove the Bowling rein and take the horse into a larger area to work.

On your first outing you should remain as relaxed and quiet as you can.

Begin at the walk and take the horse all round the riding arena on both reins, so that it knows there is nothing to fear. Then begin working through the same training programme that you used in the round pen. To your delight, you should now discover that you have a new-found ability to collect your horse. By applying a light, see-sawing action of the reins, in time with the horse's movement, to imitate the action of the Bowling rein, you should find that your horse now flexes at the poll, and brings its legs under itself to balance. Constant repetition should soon ensure that even when you cease applying the aid the horse will remain in the desired position. This will give you not only a much more pleasing outline, but also a far better balanced horse, which is ready for the manoeuvres of more advanced training.

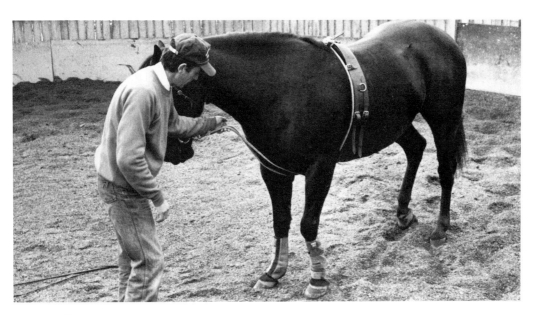

Fig 76 Initiating the rein back: I am lifting the slack out of the reins. The very moment the horse starts to move back, I will release the pressure. It is the release that gives the horse a reward for doing well. If I also praise it, it will learn to enjoy the work.

The Softly, Softly Approach

Throughout all your training it is vital that you try to remain soft and relaxed at all times. Horses are relatively timid creatures and easily become frightened and anxious. A horse that is frightened will be thinking only of escape and not what you are trying to teach it. I am sometimes asked what should be done when a horse starts to misbehave totally. How does the quiet, soft approach work then? The short answer is that it does not work! But beware my answer. You must make the distinction between wilful misbehaviour and confusion over your signals or a lack of suppleness.

To punish a horse for misbehaviour is one thing, but to punish a horse for rider error is a cardinal sin. I am told that the association time of a horse, that is the time in which it links one thing with another in its mind, is just three seconds. So, both when riding and correcting your horse, you must apply your aids and any correction promptly. Quite the best description I have ever read of how to reconcile softness with discipline is given by Dr G. F. Corley in his book *Riding and Schooling the Western Performance Horse.* He says:

Being a soft rider does not mean that they hesitate to correct a horse's mistakes for the sake of always remaining soft. Quite the contrary is true. These same soft riders are quick and efficient in punishing disobediences by the horse, but then, almost in the same breath, they can return to soft and sympathetic riding. The ability to punish a horse at exactly the instant when he will understand why he is being punished, and the ability to return to the lesson in hand almost casually is one characteristic that makes advanced riders so efficient in their schooling, and therefore successful in the show ring.

8 Building on the Basics

In all your basic schooling your guiding principle should be to ensure that the response you require from your horse is the one it finds easiest to give. Consequently you should concentrate not only on teaching your horse to respond to your aids but also on making it supple. If your horse is to find any of its training easy, it must be sufficiently fit and supple.

As I have already said, many riders are guilty of demanding that their horses perform athletically without first spending the time on making them athletes. The inability of your horse to cope with any particular manoeuvre you require may occasionally be due to its lack of comprehension, but I would estimate that 70 per cent of the time the problem is due to the horse not being sufficiently athletic or supple to attempt the manoeuvre.

Suppling Exercises

A supple horse should be able to flex easily at the poll and give to the bridle. It will be able to flex its head and neck sideways without moving its shoulders. It will also be able to move its shoulders or its hip to one side or the other whether travelling forwards or backwards. The supple horse should also be able to give you its shoulder, its ribcage and its hip without needing to use its head and neck to balance itself.

Every schooling session should therefore begin with a selection of suppling exercises designed to loosen your horse up and extend its athletic ability. Begin by asking your horse to flex at the poll and give to the bridle. To do this you need to take a light rein contact and apply gentle pressure with your fingers, squeezing the reins alternately in time with each step your horse takes at the walk. At the same time, use your seat and legs to drive the horse up.

Your horse should remember the lessons it learnt in the Bowling rein and begin to yield. The point to understand here is that the Western horse works 'off the bridle', so that when it gives its head and assumes the correct position, you must relax the rein to a small degree. The moment the horse starts to put its nose out again, you will feel the rein pressure in your fingers, whereupon you must squeeze the reins alternately until the horse gives its head again. Horses learn by repetition and reward. The relaxation of the rein is the horse's reward for placing its head and neck in the correct position.

If you do not relax the rein, the horse will begin to lean on the bit. If it leans on the bit when you use your seat and legs to drive it up, the moment you relax it will fall straight back on the forehand. Once your horse is responding reliably to leg pressure, is flexing at the poll, reining back willingly and beginning to move sideways, you can start putting a few exercises together and making the horse work harder at the walk.

Direct Bend Circles

Begin with a series of direct bend circles. As I said earlier, it is important that you visualise the line you are on, and that you keep your legs on either side of this line and your seat on top of it. You want your horse to bend its head and neck in an arc which corresponds to the line of the circle and then follow that line with its body. By visualising the circle, should your horse wander off the line, you will find that the corrective aids come to you more instinctively.

When riding circles without the support of the round pen, it will be up to you to make sure that your horse bends through its head and neck. Your horse must also stay upright through its body and maintain your chosen line accurately. Ridden well, circles provide the foundation for all Western training. (*See* Fig 77.) Although it is physically impossible for a horse to bend through its back, it is still useful to think of bending the horse around the circle, as it will make you more aware of how accurately it is following the required line.

If the horse drops its hip to the outside, you should push it back with your outside leg. If a shoulder drops out, you should again use your outside leg, but this time apply the pressure a little further forward. If a shoulder drops in, you should lightly nudge the horse back into line with your inside leg. All too often I see riders pulling one rein or the other to get back on line, only to end up riding a circle that looks more like the cog on a bicycle wheel. Once the horse is flexed at the poll and has its nose correctly bent to the inside, you should imagine that your hands are almost fixed together.

If your horse then begins to cut in, on a

Fig 77 Direct bend circle: Tewy giving her head quite happily to the right rein contact without dropping her shoulder.

left circle for example, the only way you will get it back on line is to apply a little inside seatbone and inside leg pressure to move the horse's body out. At the same time you should move both hands slightly to the right. This way you will maintain the correct neck bend. If you simply pull the right rein instead, your horse will lose its hindquarters to the inside, its shoulders will drop on one side and you will overshoot the line. You will then end up tugging on the inside rein to try to bring the horse back on course as you fishtail around the arena.

What the horse learns most clearly from this, is that it is uncomfortable to be on a circle as its shoulders are being flopped from one side to the other and its mouth is being pulled apart. Therefore, whenever your horse moves off the line of the circle, you should use your outside

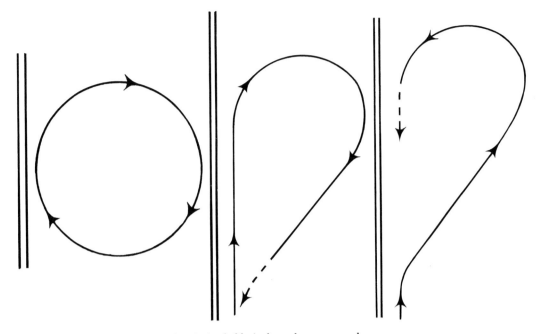

Fig 78 Schooling patterns: the circle, half-circle and reverse and the half-circle in reverse. (The latter two are typically Western ways of changing reins while schooling.)

leg to push either its barrel or hip back in again as required.

I am often asked which aids are required to maintain a perfect circle, but that is an impossible question to answer. Riding is a team game, and how successfully you play your part depends largely on your partner. So, when riding a circle, all that can be said for sure is that you must give whatever aids are required to keep your horse upright, on line and with the correct bend to its body. If you find it difficult to visualise the circle, then by all means set out some cones or similar markers. Begin by placing them just a yard apart and then, over a period of time, take every other one away. That way you will train your mind to visualise the correct line between them.

As a test of a rider's visualisation, I often trace out a circle in the floor cover-ing of our arena and then ask the rider to ride it. When he or she can ride it accurately at the walk, I ask for another circle to be ridden in the opposite direction, to give a figure of eight. (*See* Fig 80.) It can be quite revealing for the beginner to examine the result, which is usually one neat circle attached to a rather oddly shaped egg! Try it yourself. Once you have mastered it at the walk, try it at the jog.

Start with a forty-five foot (15m) circle, then a thirty-foot (10m) circle and work down to just eighteen feet (6m). Remember though, that you must keep your horse upright and balanced. During the transition from one circle to the other, the horse's head and neck must flex to the new arc before the shoulder turns. One of the commonest faults I see when riders move from one circle to another is that

Fig 79   Sheila on a three-year-old mare, nicely balanced on a canter circle, with the rider visualising the circle line.

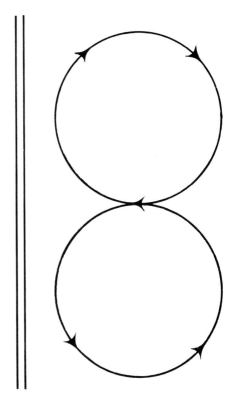

Fig 80   The figure of eight.

they forget to support the horse's shoulder with their inside leg, so that it drops its shoulder into the new circle. In other words, the horse has taken one step backwards to turning as it would do naturally out in the field and not as you require it to do to stay in balance with you, the rider.

Visualisation is also useful because it requires you to think ahead, and to ride accurately you must always be thinking ahead and anticipating your horse's movement. A top dressage rider often has just as much trouble controlling a horse as a young novice rider. The difference between them is that the experienced rider feels and corrects the faults almost before they happen.

Another mistake commonly made when riding circles, particularly at the faster paces, is to turn the horse in the same way as you would a car or a motorbike. This involves lifting the outside hand, dropping the inside hand, twisting the shoulders and perhaps even leaning to the inside. To stay in balance with your horse, however, you must stay upright and in the centre of the saddle.

If a rider suffers badly from these faults, I usually suggest that they consider holding their inside hand higher than their outside hand and that they try to sit towards the outside of the saddle. The result is that they usually end up sitting straight and balanced in the middle of the saddle, with their hands level.

When teaching your horse to ride circles out in the large arena, start big. In the early days you do not want to

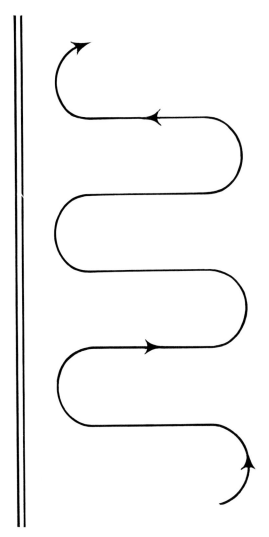

Fig 81 The serpentine.

overload your horse by asking too much and having to correct it every few strides. By starting big and progressing to smaller circles only when the horse moves in a balanced and correct way, your horse will understand better what is required of it. As with any part of the training programme, if ever you reach a point where your horse is having genuine difficulty, go back to the stage before.

Neck Reining

When riding direct bend circles, it is a good idea from time to time to lay the outside rein lightly on your horse's neck, with no bit pressure. In time your horse will begin to associate the neck rein with the correct head and neck position, and will not simply turn in from the shoulder which is a common problem when this aid is taught.

A horse that neck reins is one that will move away from rein pressure on its neck. So if you lay the right rein against its neck your horse should turn its head and neck to the left. To achieve this response takes time and you must always go quietly to a direct rein if, at any time, you feel the horse drop its shoulder and lead with it.

Neck reining, when correctly done, means that your horse is balanced through its shoulders, its ribcage and its hips. The moment any of these fall out of line, a direct rein, in conjunction with your seat and legs, must be used to correct the arc of the horse's body. In time, and with careful repetition, you will be able to lessen the use of the direct rein, but you may never abandon it completely. Like us, horses learn bad habits more easily than good ones, so it is vital that you correct any mistakes as soon as they occur.

Neck reining and riding one-handed are very commonly misunderstood parts of Western riding. As you will already have noticed, virtually all Western training and most Western riding, is actually done two-handed. This is because no horse can learn to turn and manoeuvre correctly if you have only one hand on the reins. Only on a finished horse should you attempt to ride one-handed.

Indirect Bend Circles

Once you have your horse's nose nicely tipped to the inside of your circle and it feels level, balanced and comfortable walking the line, you can try bending it in the opposite direction, on what is called an indirect bend circle.

Let us assume you are walking a direct bend circle to the right. To bend the horse indirectly, move your right hand up and across onto your horse's neck, keeping the flexion to the right. At the same time you move your weight to your left seatbone but push with your right leg. You should then see your horse move onto an indirect bend circle; that is, with its shoulder to the inside and its head to the outside.

The first few times you try this, do not make the circle so small as to be difficult for your horse. You should also be aware that, on the indirect bend circle, the horse will probably still want to move its head to the inside of the circle, so be very light with your hands and use little checks and releases to help the horse to understand your wishes, not a constant pressure. You will probably feel the horse become a little unsteady and lose its 1-2-3-4 rhythm at the walk. Keep the circle large until it regains its balance and rhythm before attempting to make the circle smaller or the flexion too great.

Remember, your ultimate goal must be to keep your horse moving softly and with a steady, regular rhythm to its hoofbeats, irrespective of where you place its head and neck. You will only achieve this when your horse is both supple and balanced. Avoid the temptation to use the reins in an effort to control its movement around the circle. Remember that your horse will move

Fig 82 Indirect bend circle: I have quietly moved my right hand up across her neck and put my weight into my left seatbone. She immediately moves over to the left, crossing her front legs, staying relaxed even though her head is to the outside.

under weight transference and away from leg pressure; he does not want a trip to the dentist! Applying too much rein can also have the undesirable effect of overfacing the horse and blocking its shoulder movement.

So work slowly and quietly, and concentrate on achieving that steady rhythm of the hoofbeats. When you do you will know that your horse is not dropping its ribcage into the turn, as this would shorten its inside stride, but that it is responding to your aids and staying reasonably level.

More Circle Training

Another exercise you can practise while riding circles is to turn your horse's head to the inside and then drop your inside leg further back along the flank, and ask the horse to yield its hip. You should then be able to push it around, making it cross its rear legs while still maintaining forward motion. If at any time your horse speeds up, or you lose its shoulders to the outside as it tries to evade the pressure of your leg, use your outside rein to block its escape.

Push Offs

From direct bend circles and figures of eight you can progress to what I call 'push offs'. In this you ask your horse to move off the circle and work down the side of the arena while keeping its head and neck arced to the inside as you push it in a straight line with your inside leg. Push offs teach the horse to allow you to control its shoulder, hip and barrel while moving in a straight line with its head and neck slightly arced to the inside. If you push off alongside a hedge or fence, your horse will resist the natural temptation to swing its hip out. It will feel supported by the barrier and so will find the exercise easier.

Take care not to overbend the horse's nose and make it all too uncomfortable for it. Take your time. Remember, you are asking the horse to do something that is a little difficult and uncomfortable for it, and, while it will want to please you, if you overdo it, it will resist and rebel.

The Two-Track

The next suppling exercise I like to teach a horse is the two-track or leg yield. You should train your horse to yield to leg pressure without speeding up. Two-tracking teaches this together with the basics of a good sidepass. It also helps to reinforce the bond of trust between you, as the horse learns that it can cross its legs over without fear.

The best way to teach the two-track or leg yield is to find a convenient hedge or fence to ride down. Assuming the fence is on your left, you should ride alongside it for a few strides and then gently turn your horse's nose towards it. With your left hand just feeling its mouth, apply some pressure with your left leg to move its body out. Do not ask for too much to start with and always practise both ways, to the left and to the right.

What you are trying to achieve is for your horse to cross its front and hindlegs over. What usually happens at first, however, is that the horse tends to go straight, with just its head and neck bent. So, when going to the left, put a little weight in your right rein and you should then feel the horse's body straighten while still moving on a slight diagonal. If you find this difficult, try turning your toe out a little and keeping the left leg long, so that the weight of your hip is on the side away from the direction of travel. The horse will then try to establish its centre of gravity between you both. This should clarify your intentions and will help the horse. Remember, however, that you are not trying to overpower the horse but actually to make it easy for it to achieve what you wish.

If this sounds confusing, think about how you would move yourself sideways.

Fig 83 Tewy staying straight through her neck and body as she two-tracks.

Imagine that you are standing still with your legs slightly apart, and that you want to move sideways to the right. You would first put your weight into your left leg, take your right leg off the ground and then push off the left. Assume this position in the saddle and your horse will move away from the pressure. You should feel that your seatbone is taking the horse in the direction you require.

When applying leg aids, remember to apply pressure with the whole of your leg. Many novices draw the heel up, which takes the knee away and so the leg becomes soft, weak and ineffective.

If there is a convenient corner to the hedge or fence, you can work right up to this. On approaching the corner, the horse should be at a 45-degree angle to it. By pushing with your right leg behind the girth, your horse should move away from the pressure and will start to move in the opposite direction. Because the right leg is securing the hip the horse will begin a turn on the haunches, whereupon you can two-track in the opposite direction.

Two-tracking should first be practised at the walk and then at the jog. To begin with, accept the barest minimum of sideways movement and work up from there. At the completion of any exercise which your horse has performed well, give it a chance to stand square and rest. You can even work on the horse's suppleness while in this resting position by gently lifting one rein and then the other, so that the horse tips its nose from side to side. All the time it does this, however, it must keep its shoulders upright and square.

To begin with, the movement will be minimal. With practice, however, as the horse becomes increasingly supple, you should be able to take its nose right round to the toe of your boot on either side. When you can do this without the horse resisting, stepping out or twisting its shoulders, then you are on the way to owning a horse that is supple in its head and neck.

Refining the Rein Back

Having taught your horse to rein back a step or two, you should now begin to ask for a more positive back up. After asking for the halt, keep the weight down in your heels and your lower back rounded and take a light contact on the reins. Cluck and ask your horse to back verbally. If you get the step back, release the pressure, sit back in the centre of the saddle and praise your horse. Once it has relaxed for a moment, walk on, halt and rein back again. This time insist on a second step. It should not be too long before your horse will rein back as many steps as you require.

Be sure to put your weight right down in your heels and to round your lower back. If you work hard on these aids, then your horse will eventually rein back without any use of the reins whatsoever. If your horse resists the rein back, do not pull harder on the reins. Instead, reach forward with one or other leg and lightly tap the horse on its shoulder. This usually persuades the horse to lift one leg, and if you maintain a gentle pressure on the reins, it will almost certainly step backwards.

I appreciate that this might sound a little strange to some people, but believe me it works without you having to apply extra rein pressure. It is a much better training technique than having someone on the ground pushing and shoving the horse in the chest. It is also far preferable to the rider yanking away at the reins. After all, a horse backs with his legs not his teeth!

The idea of riders rounding their backs and pushing their heels down may also sound strange. However, if the horse backs correctly by lowering its croup, getting its hocks underneath it and elevating its shoulders, then the rider will give the appearance of staying in the centre of the saddle.

Rein Backs on the Circle

Once your horse is reining back readily without resistance, you can ask for its hip just as you did when going forward. Do this by dropping your weight onto your right seatbone, then draw your right leg back and ask the horse to give its hip to the left. You should then be able to ride a circle in reverse. In order to do this, however, you must have a light inside rein pressure and you should hold the rein close to the horse's neck. You may also need to apply the opposite leg at the girth, to stop the shoulder from falling in. Your horse will discover that it has two ways of getting away from your leg pressure. It can drop a shoulder to the inside and so straighten its body and escape the pressure of your outside leg. Or it can turn its head and neck to the outside and so twist its body away from the leg pressure.

The purpose of the exercise is to make sure you keep the horse's head, neck and shoulders straight and that it moves its hip over. Your goal should be to work towards a position whereby you can take your horse's hip to the right simply by putting your weight down and applying the outside leg, so that the horse makes a circle backwards to the right. You should then immediately be able to centre your body so that the horse now backs straight for a few paces, and then, by dropping your weight onto the other side and applying the other leg, the horse should promptly and willingly back a circle in the other direction.

This manoeuvre is particularly important as a foundation exercise for canter departures and, more important, for flying lead changes. A lead change is simply the result of moving the horse's hip from one side to the other, while keeping its shoulders in a straight line.

Upward Transitions

When you feel that your horse has become balanced and supple at the walk, you can try the same exercises in trot and canter. At the same time you should also be working towards achieving the soft smooth Western paces of the jog and lope. Unless your horse has learnt to go forward and engage its hindquarters properly, it is never going to perform the jog and lope correctly. Remember, the slowness of the Western horse is attained through increased engagement and not by the rider pulling on the reins. Increasing rein contact more often only results in a 'jig', a lazy trot, or a four-beat canter.

The correct Western jog has a beautiful softness to it, retaining the 'floatability' of the dressage horse, together with a slightly shorter stride. Similarly, the lope is a comfortable rocking gait. The jog and lope can only be achieved once the trot and canter have been attained with good engagement. To move up from the walk to the trot, urge your horse forward by closing both legs softly against its sides, clucking or kissing to him and allowing a little flexibility in the poll. You have to teach the horse not to run into the trot or canter, but to engage deeper and rebalance itself for the new gait.

When trotting, you should assume the same rising position as the English-style rider. Similarly, when cantering there is no significant difference in the rider's position, which should be upright but relaxed, with a soft lower back so that the pelvic movement absorbs the motion. Many English-style riders get used to standing in their stirrups when they canter, allowing the top half of their body to flow up and down. Consequently, when they sit, they tend to bob about like

plastic ducks. This has the effect of urging the horse forward with their shoulders. Ideally they should relax the lower back, so that any change of pace can come from the seat.

When you lean your body forward you are putting weight on the forehand, which will drive the horse on. This is because the speed of a horse is governed by its ability to move its front legs, not its hind legs. No matter how powerful your horse may be, it cannot go fast unless it can get its front legs out of the way speedily. In our transition up to canter there is the further complication of establishing the correct sequence of legs and the right lead. If you think of a person skipping along, as their left leg leads, their left hip comes forward, and as their right leg leads, their right hip is forward. Try to reverse this natural process and you will feel very uncomfortable indeed.

So, when we ask a horse in its early training to canter, we do it on a circle and we move the horse's hip to the inside of our line by using our outside leg, while holding its head and shoulders square. The horse is now effectively 'leading' with its inside hip, so that when we apply a little extra pressure and ask for the canter, the horse will lead with its inside foreleg simply because it is easiest for it to do so.

An even simpler way to grasp this notion is to think of the horse as a rather wobbly table. If you sit down hard on the rear right corner of the table, it should be obvious that the leg which will first come off the ground will be the left front. Eventually, your horse will learn to move into canter at the merest hint of pressure from your outside leg, while keeping its body straight. Proof of this comes with the ability of a horse quite early on in its training to go from walk to canter with the minimum of fuss.

Downward Transitions

When you first asked your horse to rein back, you asked it to elevate its shoulders and to bring its hocks underneath it. This is exactly the same response you require when asking for a downward transition. You want the horse to engage a little deeper behind so that it moves its centre of gravity rearwards and balances itself as it changes gait and slows down.

Just as when a car slows quickly you must brace yourself or you will fall forward, so the horse and rider must balance themselves against the inertia which would otherwise tip them forward. It should be obvious, therefore, that having asked our horse to rein back correctly, we should apply similar aids, but more lightly, to achieve a smooth downward transition. The transition down from the trot to the walk is asked for simply by rounding up the lower back, putting more weight in our heels and moving our lower leg slightly forwards. The horse soon learns to recognise this signal and will make the transition down to walk without the need for us to pull on the reins; all we need do then is balance its head with them.

More often than not you will find that your horse will come to a stop, rather than a walk. This means you have rather overdone your cues. Personally, I find this fault more desirable than when a horse just falls into walk on the forehand. At least your horse has responded with greater engagement, and it also implies that you have achieved some lightness of control in that you can effect such a dramatic change of pace simply through the use of your seat and a change in your body position.

For the transition from canter to trot, the same aids apply. Again, concentrate on achieving greater engagement and you will avoid the problem of your horse crashing from a canter into a trot on the forehand. As your horse grows accustomed to recognising these cues, you will be able to half-halt it at any time simply by dropping a little weight into the stirrups. This suggests to the horse that it should engage its hindquarters a little deeper and so it will adopt a softer pace. From this you should also begin to appreciate yourself just how much influence you can have on your horse simply through your seat and body position.

Rein Aids

The harder you work on your transitions and the use of your seat and body aids, the further you will progress from the 'kick to start, pull to stop' school of riding. Although a finished horse should be able to perform any manoeuvre from a spin to a sliding stop even without a bridle, the reins do, however, have a valuable part to play.

The reins should complement the leg and seat aids. Not only do we want the horse simply to give to the bridle, we want it to understand the five different rein aids that we will use in our schooling. To apply rein aids properly, it is important that the rider is in the correct position and is supple enough to absorb the horse's motion while keeping his or her hands independent.

The three most familiar rein aids are

the bearing rein, or neck rein, where the rein is laid lightly on the horse's neck and from which it moves away; a leading rein, which is a direct rein out towards one side, which the horse follows with its nose; and a direct rein of opposition, where both reins are drawn back, causing the horse to stop, collect itself or rein back. Two other rein aids, which are often forgotten, are the direct rein of opposition, in which one hand moves up and forward in front of the saddle horn to move the horse's shoulder away from the rein; and a direct rein of opposition behind the saddle horn and towards the rider's hip, which helps the horse to move its hip in the opposite direction. Here you can see straightaway that to lock your hands firmly into one 'correct' position is entirely wrong and would limit your ability to school the horse effectively. Instead, you must be soft with your hands and use the rein aids in support of your weight transference and leg aids to achieve the effect you desire.

When asking a horse to perform any particular task, you must do whatever is necessary to get the job done. If you need to use your legs, seat and reins to obtain the required result, then use all three. However, if you can build into your training system an approach whereby you trust your horse to do what is required, and then help it by correcting it quietly and simply as you proceed each step of the way, you will find the horse very quickly learns what you require. Trusting a horse and being as light as possible with the aids, are the two things I find most difficult to persuade many riders to attempt.

Rein aids, above all, must be applied with care and feel. Considering the importance of this, it is ridiculous how few riders actually practise something as simple as picking up the slack in a rein slowly until they can feel the contact before giving a rein aid. Horses do not respond like switches, but through feel. It is this feel and understanding which enable a good rider to get on a bad horse and make it look good. Conversely, a lack of feel will result in a bad rider destroying a good horse within a few rides.

Preparing Your Horse for the Trail

Once you have familiarised your horse with the suppling exercises of circles, push offs, two-tracking, rollbacks and turns on the forehand and haunches, it is time to introduce it to some of the objects to be found in a Western Trail Class. I do this not simply as a preparation for competition but because a horse that readily and willingly accepts obstacles in your arena will be far safer out on the roads and tracks. I am often appalled to see horses out on the road which do not even respond to the rider's legs aids and which cannot move sideways or backwards, let alone cope with unfamiliar hazards and obstacles calmly and safely.

It should be common sense, however, not to venture out on the road before you have established these basic controls in the peace and quiet of an arena. Furthermore, your horse must be trained to trust you so that should you meet anything new or frightening out on the road, it will allow you to reassure it rather than respond horse style, by turning to flee at the gallop.

Fig 84 *A four-year-old stallion standing quietly by the side of a gate.*

Trail Obstacles

The first trail obstacle to work on is the one most commonly encountered out on a hack – the gate. Your objective should be to train your horse to approach a gate in such a way that, from the saddle, you can open, ride through and close the gate in perfect control and with the gateway blocked at all times so that if there is any stock in the field, none can escape.

To achieve this, your horse must first sidepass up to the gate and stand still while you unlatch the gate. It must then rein back, allowing you to slide your hand back towards the hinge. As you push the gate away, you should apply a little outside leg pressure so that the horse turns on its haunches and walks through

the gateway. As it does this, you can slide your hand back along the gate, halting your horse when it is back at the latch. A further 45-degree turn on the forehand should allow you to draw the gate back into the closed position. A final turn on the haunches and you should now be in a position finally to relatch the gate. (*See* Figs 84 to 88.)

This may sound a rather long-winded process, but tackled calmly and smoothly it is actually quite quick. This fact was proved conclusively by my wife Sheila when competing in hunter trials. She negotiated a gate far quicker using this technique than all the other riders who galloped up to it and then spent the next ten minutes trying to quieten their horses sufficiently to reach the latch.

Fig 85 *After releasing the latch and backing a couple of strides, Sheila has initiated the turn on the haunches and proceeds through the gate.*

Fig 86 *At the latch end of the gate Sheila pauses and makes a turn on the forehand to clear the gate.*

107

Fig 87 All that Sheila has to do now is move the gate past her leg, make a final 45-degree turn on the haunches, and she will be in a position to close and latch the gate.

Fig 88 Closing the gate.

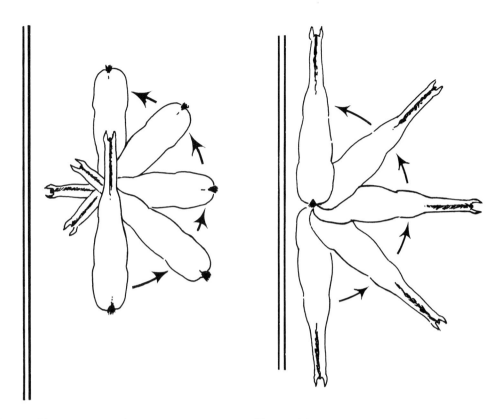

Fig 89 Turning on the forehand.

Fig 90 Turning on the haunches.

You should also take your horse over obstacles such as noisy surfaces made to simulate bridges. That way the horse will learn that such obstacles are not dangerous and not to be feared. I must stress that here you must work very softly and slowly, particularly if you are schooling a young horse. You should always stop before an obstacle and stand there for a while to let your horse get a good look at it. It is also a good idea to walk around an obstacle a few times, on both reins, so that the horse has a clear picture of it from every angle. In some cases, when training a young horse, it may even be best for you to lead it through an obstacle by hand on the first occasion. With an obstacle such as a bridge, you should step onto it, and then stop and let your horse

relax. Let it consider where it is and realise that there is nothing to fear.

Another trail obstacle to work on is a ground pole over which you must side-pass. Using a pole will enable you to practise this useful manoeuvre with a little more accuracy. Here you should concentrate especially on stopping your horse stepping forwards or backwards. Various pole arrangements can also be laid down through which you have to rein back and turn. Again, this sharpens your control and teaches the horse to respond correctly to your leg aids.

Your horse should also become accustomed to you putting on and taking off brightly coloured and noisy waterproofs, to spectators opening and closing umbrellas and to large scary vehicles like

109

Fig 91 The horse (Keo) showing good concentration on the bridge obstacle. He has put his head down to inspect the obstacle, ensuring that he will be able to step onto it carefully.

Fig 92 Having decided it is safe to cross, Keo makes the crossing in a calm and relaxed manner.

Fig 93 The horse leaves the obstacle slowly and without a trace of worry – the ideal type of horse to hack out on. This horse is only four, and has only been backed for twelve months.

tractors and horse boxes. Again, the young horse can be introduced to these things at a very early age while being led out on walks.

All my horses, whether schooled English or Western, and for whatever discipline, must be able to cope with these trail class obstacles. I find no pleasure at all in riding a horse that is easily spooked or which will not respond accurately to leg pressure. The correct response to leg pressure is vital in gaining a horse's confidence to overcome any problem.

9 Advanced Western Schooling

If you have worked steadily through your Western training programme, you should already be enjoying riding a better schooled, better balanced and much safer horse. Many weekend riders often feel that this is as far as they want to go. Even if you have no plans to go Reining, however, there is no reason why you should not continue schooling your horse and introduce it to some of the more advanced Western techniques.

Lead Changes

For a horse to change direction smoothly at the canter or lope, it must be able to change leads at your command. Such changes are called flying changes. They can be achieved quite easily by putting a correctly balanced horse into a position where switching leads becomes the most comfortable thing for it to do.

When you ask for a canter departure, you keep your horse's shoulders, head and neck straight and use your outside leg to push its hip to the inside. The resulting pressure causes the horse to step up into canter, and because of the way you have controlled its body, it will pick up the correct lead. As well as through your canter departures, you should also have reinforced this lesson by teaching your horse to give you its hip in either direction while backing up.

You can test your control of the horse's hip at any time while walking forward, by asking the horse to yield its hip to one side and then to the other, at the same time making sure its shoulder does not fall in. I like to walk an imaginary line down the centre of the arena, concentrating on keeping my horse's shoulder and neck straight as I move its hip to either side of the line. The result is not unlike the dressage movement of travers.

When you are ready to start lead changing, you should begin by working on a circle of about sixty feet (20m). At the centre point, stop your horse, sidepass a few steps to the inside of the circle, then push with your new outside leg and move the horse out on the opposite circle at the canter. This exercise will help to teach your horse to adapt to each new lead in a relaxed manner. When it can move from just a few steps of walk into a canter on the correct lead, you can begin to make your circle slightly pear-shaped. As you canter along the straighter edge of your pear shape, begin to turn your horse's head to the outside. Keep the horse's outside shoulder up and the inside shoulder dropped. Having achieved this control over its shoulder, turn the horse back into the circle, allow it to adopt the correct head and neck and hold its shoulders square.

The horse will probably find this exercise uncomfortable and if you have not worked hard enough at your suppling exercises, in particular the direct and

Fig 94 On the right lead, I begin to take some rein contact to help elevate the horse's front end. I am also applying a little left leg pressure to move its shoulders slightly to the right.

Fig 95 As the horse vaults over the original leading (right) leg, I begin to use my right leg to move its hip over to the left, releasing the shoulder from my left leg.

Fig 96 *As I sit a little lighter, the horse has already responded by placing the right hind leg down first. The ease with which the horse does this can be seen by the slack in the reins. The head is up, but it is better that the horse learns this way first.*

Fig 97 *The horse completes the change, finding it the most comfortable thing to do – now praise the horse!*

114

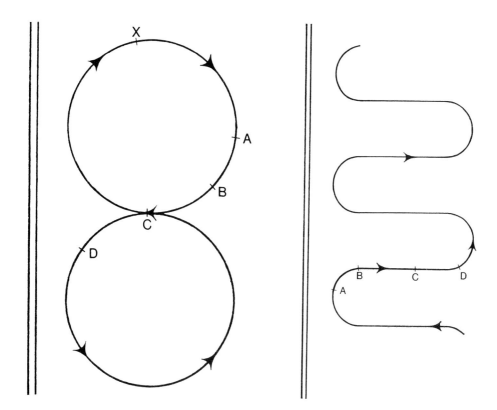

Fig 98 Lead changes on a figure of eight and serpentine.

indirect bend circles, then you will find the horse resisting you. You must eliminate any stiffness from your horse's poll and neck for this exercise to work. Furthermore, any stiffness must be eliminated at the walk before you progress to the trot and canter. When your horse will accept this manoeuvre without resistance, ride the straighter side of your pattern with the horse's nose tipped to the outside and its shoulder moved across to the inside. Then ask your horse to move its hip to the outside, using your inside leg and seatbone.

At the same time as you do this, give the outside rein slightly, so that the horse can straighten its head, and, if you leave your leg at the girth, you will find that your horse will change leads. It may also

speed up, but do not slow it down with the reins. This is a new experience for the horse and you do not want to give it unpleasant associations. This technique may seem a little strange to English riders who have learnt 'drop to trot' changes, but it works very efficiently as is proved by the ease with which Western horses accept lead changes at such an early age.

If you allow your horse's shoulder to drop, however, or its head to dive to the inside of the new circle, then you will lose the chance of changing leads. This usually occurs when the rider waits until he or she is too close to the side of the arena and then twists his or her body to the inside of the corner. This has the effect of letting the horse's new inside shoulder drop, for the rider's new inside leg has moved back, and the horse's hip will swing out. The result is a horse which is disunited for it will change at the front but not at the back. To prevent this you must keep control of the horse's shoulder, ribcage and hip.

If the horse does not change, maintain the new circle, keep its nose tipped to the inside, its inside shoulder up, and keep pushing the hip. Normally the horse will break to trot itself and then pick up the new lead almost immediately, because it has understood your canter signal aid. When practising this technique, some riders overbend the horse's neck, causing the inside shoulder to drop. Watch out for this. You must also ensure that your leg aid is effective enough to push the hip over while your other leg and your hands remain soft, so that the horse's shoulders and head do not move out of position.

Very often any problems which are encountered with flying changes can be traced to the rider not doing his or her homework correctly and perhaps not securing the horse's hip properly. Your horse will find it very difficult to canter on a right lead with its hip hanging out to the left. If you do your part correctly, what you will be doing is making the original lead uncomfortable for your horse and the new one inviting. I always try to sit a little lighter as I ask for a lead change, for the horse is going to have to lift its back a touch more than normal, and I do not want to hinder it. Horses trained correctly in this way usually learn to do flying changes in quite a short space of time and in a relaxed manner.

A word of warning, however! When you have achieved a clean change on both leads, do not rush on to one-time changes to show off. Lead changing is hard work for a horse and you do not want it to

dread it. Work slowly. Horses do not drop back to trot to change leads out in the field, so you are working naturally with your horse. However, you are insisting that it works to your command, and the horse will find this taxing. So, when you have completed a few good changes, praise your horse, let it relax and then move on to something new.

If you find that your horse is actually trying to anticipate you, rather than working in response to your aids, ride a few canter circles until you have its full attention once more. Taught carefully, the novice horse will soon be doing five-time changes, which is about the most a Western horse is ever asked to do, in a straight line and in a relaxed manner.

The Spin

The spin is an advanced Western technique, involving one or more 360-degree turns, with the horse pivoting on the inside hind leg while crossing over his front legs. At no time do you want your horse to hop around his pivot leg. A spin should be flat and smooth. From your work on two-tracking and the 180-degree turns on the haunches, you have already laid the foundations for the spin. Your horse will have learnt both to cross over in front and to plant a rear leg when turning. If your horse cannot perform either of these manoeuvres correctly, do not attempt the spin.

To train your horse to spin, begin by riding a thirty-foot (10m) circle at the walk. Pay particular attention to keeping the horse upright. If it can handle a circle of that size easily enough, slowly make it smaller. Keep an inside leg at the girth at all times, to stop the horse's inside shoul-

Fig 99 A spin without a bit: Dick Pieper demonstrating a spin on Enterprise Velvet. Velvet's (left) shoulder is upright as she reaches with her near fore, pivoting around her near hind leg. (Photograph by Valerie Parry.)

der dropping and its barrel rotating. Either of these faults will prevent you from achieving a flat spin.

If the shoulder drops and the barrel rotates, the inside leg will hit the ground and take a shorter stride than the outside leg. Your horse will then try to compensate for this and start hopping. The other problem you can encounter, is that when you draw the circle down, instead of crossing in front, your horse will slap or kick one of its legs. In this case, it will either not plant a pivot leg or it may try to back out of the spin. If it starts kicking

itself, it will certainly not reach across in front, and again it may start to hop.

The answer is to practise repeatedly walking the circles down in size. When your horse finally discovers that it is actually more comfortable to cross in front, then you can tighten the circle still further and suggest that it plants a rear leg. Encourage your horse by sitting back a little and putting extra weight on your inside seatbone. Lay the outside rein on the neck, guide the horse with the inside rein and gently push and nudge it with your outside leg. If the horse plants

117

Figs 100–106 *Alice (April Workman) came to us as a five-year-old to re-establish her spin and improve it. The sequence is a good one: the pivot foot locked into place, the outside hind leg driving around, and Alice staying flat and soft in the bridle.*

its inside hindleg and gives you even half a turn to start with, praise it and walk it out.

You can now build on this by walking down the outside of the arena, turning the horse towards the fence and then pushing it round the next 90 degrees. The fence will help you by preventing the horse from moving forwards. When it can manage this 180-degree turn, walk down the fence again. This time, however, ask the horse to pivot 180 degrees to the inside. Having completed the turn, push the horse through the next 180 degrees towards the fence, to complete the full turn. Remember that the spin is basically forward motion with the outside foreleg reaching across and in front of the inside foreleg. Do not overdo your spin training and allow your horse plenty of time to relax.

Eventually, you will be able to start to walk a thirty-foot (10m) circle and, at the same point every time, turn your horse a

119

Fig 107 *My top Reining mare, Diablo Ima Tewlip, has shifted her weight onto her near hind leg and has flattened to begin the spin. Note the lightness of the rein contact, illustrating that she is completely relaxed in the manoeuvre.*

Fig 108 *Again showing relaxation: the front legs are crossing over correctly, with no hopping and the pivot leg is 'drilling a hole'.*

full 360 degrees on its pivot leg. At first you should not worry whether the pivot foot stays planted, or whether the horse lifts it occasionally. What is important is that the horse can walk this tight circle around its hindleg with a degree of comfort. When the horse can manage one smooth flat turn, ask for two complete turns and then walk back out onto the circle and let the horse relax. You should build to three and four turns slowly. After each spin move back out onto the circle.

If you rush this part of your spin training, you will find that your horse will begin to lose its back end and not pivot correctly, or, worse still, it will dread the spin and try to rush it to get it over with quickly. At a much later stage, when your horse thinks nothing of a four-turn spin in either direction, you can begin to use your outside leg as an accelerator, holding the hip a little and pushing in.

In a correct spin the horse's body will be straight, its head and neck will be just slightly tipped to the inside and it will remain flat and calm. If your horse starts dragging a shoulder, a gentle nudge here with your outside leg should remind it to move the shoulder a little quicker. Too often riders tap the shoulder to increase spin speed. While this can have the desired effect, beware, for while your horse may move its shoulder a little faster one way, it may lose its hip just as quickly the other way. The result is a horse which turns about its centre and not over its pivot leg.

Another common mistake is to pull the horse round with the inside rein. This invariably results in the hip being lost to the outside, quite the opposite effect to

Fig 109 *A close-up of the left hind pivot leg and the mare's front legs crossing correctly.*

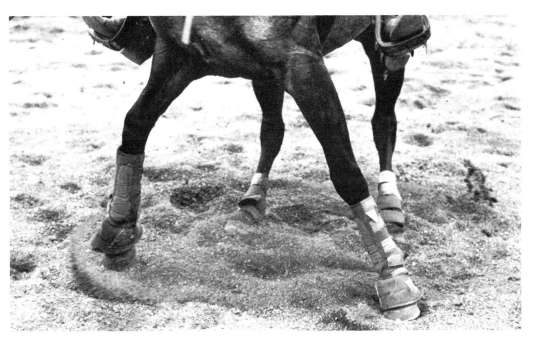

Fig 110 *A spin to the right: Tewy showing her remarkable ability to stretch the inside foreleg.*

*Fig 111 Everything going wrong: trying to make a
horse spin and not allowing it to! The rider is pulling on
the reins; the horse's head is up; there is too much outside
contact; the head is to the outside, the horse's shoulders
have dropped and her back has hollowed.*

the one we desire. Remember, to spin properly, your horse must seek the turn on its own, while you must push it rather than pull it. Furthermore, it is useful to remember that a finished horse will spin with no rein aids whatsoever. Regular practice of direct and indirect bend circles will provide the correct foundation for this manoeuvre, as not only will this make your horse supple, but it will train it to listen to your seat and legs.

The Rollback

The rollback is a 180-degree turn over the haunches. Performed correctly, your horse should stop from the canter, turn over a pivot leg and move away at the canter on the same line it entered. Your horse will have done its first rollback when free schooled in the roundpen. From there, the turn on the haunches at the walk and the two-track can be seen as steps towards the complete manoeuvre.

An effective way of teaching your horse to rollback is to take a corner of your arena or field, and bisect the corner with an imaginary line. Ride a circle to one side of the corner and the bisecting line, say to the right. When your horse feels balanced riding that circle at the trot, leave the circle on the imaginary line at 45 degrees to the corner. When you reach the corner lift the slack out of the reins, say 'whoa' and sit down. The corner will help, but the horse should immediately bring its hocks under it and stand square.

Fig 112 Tewlip coming to a nice balanced halt, holding the slide with her hind legs, while staying free at the front.

123

Fig 113 Starting to turn: her off-side hind leg is already planted and the front off-side leg is beginning to step across.

Fig 114 Coming round nicely in the 180-degree turn.

Fig 115 The turn is nearly completed and the drive, to lope out in the opposite direction, is beginning.

Fig 116 The turn is completed and we are loping off in the opposite direction over our slide tracks with no resistance – the sign of a nicely balanced rollback.

You then quickly make a left turn by tipping the horse's nose to the left, releasing your left leg from the horse's side, so that some weight falls into the right hip, inclining your body very slightly forward and, at the same time, pushing with your right leg behind the girth. Provided that you do not pull the inside rein, but only push with your outside leg, your horse should pivot about its hindleg and turn out at the trot. You should then ride a small circle on the opposite side of the imaginary line and repeat the exercise in the opposite direction.

When you are ready to take this a step further, ride a large circle at the trot and stop six feet (2m) from the edge of the arena. Guide your horse through the first part of your rollback turn, as before, continuing the leg pressure until you make the 180-degree turn, and push the horse back out at a trot. Working on the rollback is a very useful revision exercise for your horse. It reminds it to stop at the word 'whoa', to move promptly away from leg pressure and to engage its hindquarters.

When your horse has mastered the rollback at the trot, you can repeat the exercise at the canter. You are already applying outside leg pressure on the turn, so, by increasing this slightly, your horse should move straight off into canter on the correct lead. After working for a while in the corner, and then against a fence, you should eventually be able to perform perfect rollbacks at the canter down the centre line of the arena.

You should attempt to do this at a very early stage in your horse's training as it will teach it to turn over its haunches and collect itself. Your horse must be fit, however, so do not practise this manoeuvre until you have your horse fully fit and well legged up, or you will cause unnecessary strain.

Do not assume that because the Western paces are slow and the style of riding is relaxed, you can ride Western on an unsound or unfit horse. Not only will an unfit horse find any work difficult and so less enjoyable, but performing some of the more advanced manoeuvres which you will require of your horse, will demand a high degree of athleticism which must be achieved through a regular fitness training programme.

Sliding Stop

The sliding stop is undoubtedly one of the most exciting parts of a reining display. To watch the fastest accelerating horse in the world hurtle up the arena and then slide over thirty feet (10m) in a cloud of dust in response to the lightest of aids, is to see the culmination of Western training. It must be remembered, however, that the sliding stop is very much an artificial addition to the repertoire of a working horse, developed purely as part of a reining display. The result is certainly dramatic, but the sliding stop is in no way a practical manoeuvre, and the cutting horse which slid thirty feet (10m) on every turn would soon be out of a job!

The sliding stop should only be attempted on suitably friable surfaces, usually dry clay or tarmac, covered with two to three inches (5–8cm) of sea sand or a proprietary surface such as Pasada. The horse must also be specially shod at the rear, with flat sliding plates. These should be about three-quarters of an inch (18mm) wide to begin with, moving up to one inch (25mm) wide as your horse becomes more finished. As well as splint

Fig 117 World champion Morgan Lybbert performing a
sliding stop.

boots on the forelegs, the horse should
also wear skid boots to protect the fetlock
area from friction burns.

As part of your training for the rollback, you will have taught your horse to
stop from the trot and canter by responding to your voice, rein, seat and leg aids.
Your horse should stop by getting its
hocks right under it, and this is the basis
of the sliding stop. For the sliding stop,
your horse must get both hindlegs under
it, round its loins and elevate its
shoulders. It should be totally relaxed in
the bridle and be quite willing to flex at
the poll. When your horse will stop in
this way for the rollback, you can proceed to fencing him.

Canter your horse quietly from one

end of the arena to the other and ride it
right up to the fence. As you approach
the fence, the horse is going to start
doubting your sanity and will perhaps
begin to duck and weave. To counter
this, you should maintain an equal pressure in both reins, but do not pull on the
reins in an attempt to straighten the horse.
Instead, you must use your legs to guide
it. This is vitally important, as your horse
will never stop correctly if it is not
perfectly straight from nose to tail.

As you approach the fence, you must
adopt the mental approach that you are
going to ride straight through to the
other side. Just before you make contact,
however, sit down, round up your lower
back, take your legs a little forward, with

127

Fig 118 A balanced stop on April Workman – the rein contact is minimal and the horse is light in front.

the weight in your heels, and, without taking any more of a contact on the mouth, say 'whoa'. Then trust your horse to make the decision to stop.

Begin at a slow canter and increase your speed a little each time. Do not let the horse charge from one end of the arena to the other. If it does become a little overexcited, either pull it up in the first couple of strides and back it, or ride down the side but, instead of sliding, turn it in a circle and ride a few laps of the arena until it settles down. Then try fencing it from the opposite end.

You are trying to persuade your horse to adopt the familiar position of the unsuccessful puissance horse, who, having decided not to jump the wall, puts on all the brakes at once. By not pulling on the reins in these early stages, you will encourage your horse not to jam its front legs into the ground, which might hurt it, but to round its loins, get its hindlegs underneath it, and stay free at the front.

As with any advanced technique, to do it well your horse must do it willingly. It should look forward to sliding as a good game. You should be aware, though, that sliding puts an immense amount of strain on the legs and quarters, and while a perfectly fit Western horse can manage this manoeuvre with no problem, an old, unsound or poorly conformed horse should never be stopped in this manner.

Once your horse is correctly shod, you can increase the speed of your run down,

Fig 119 Fencing: from our rollbacks the horse has understood how to get its hocks underneath it in a relaxed manner. Fencing takes it a stage further. The fence allows the horse to get both legs underneath it, and the rider just balances the horse to keep it straight. By not pulling on the reins I allow the horse to teach itself to come to the stop while staying free at the front end.

teaching the horse to build speed from a relaxed canter to a controlled gallop, but do not allow it to launch into a flat-out hell-for-leather sprint. As your horse begins to get its hocks underneath it more, you can begin to ask for the stop a little further from the fence. If your horse has learnt the technique correctly, it will gets its rear legs underneath it and the flat shoes will allow the feet to slide. By keeping your hands steady and not pulling on your horse's mouth as it digs in at the rear, you will not halt all its forward motion and its front legs will paddle forward. The combination of front legs walking and rear legs sliding makes for the perfect sliding stop. The less the rider appears to be doing the better.

You do, however, need to take the slack out of the reins and have a slight contact when stopping, to help the horse balance and elevate its shoulders. If it begins to run through the bridle, you may have to catch it and rein back saying 'whoa', to remind it that the word 'whoa' means 'get the back legs under'.

Do not expect too much too soon, and do not practise too many stops in one go, or you will burn your horse out. Fast stops and slides are extremely strenuous,

Fig 120 *Tewy is in the ground and sliding, yet the front end is clearly shown staying free and continuing to move. The rein pressure is minimal, just balancing her head, and she is flexed at the poll.*

Fig 121 Another slide; Tewy is down in the ground, straight and relaxed.

and even the fittest of horses must be given plenty of time after each stop to fill up on air and relax. Six stops per session is usually enough, after which you should walk your horse to the centre of the arena and allow it to recover fully.

In a lot of the reining competition patterns you are asked for a hesitation in the centre of the arena to show a relaxed horse. So, to pause here is useful training, as your horse will begin to associate the centre of the arena with these rest periods and not as the place from where exciting things begin. You really need to allow at least twelve months of training to build up to an impressive sliding stop if you are not to overload your horse and either injure it or simply hit a wall of resistance.

A good horse, like Diablo Ima Tewlip, on the right surface, can maintain a slide for over thirty feet (10m). Remember, however, it is the horse which maintains the stop; the rider simply initiates it with the lightest of aids. I cannot over-emphasise that a properly trained horse should stop at the word 'whoa', and the extra weight in the rider's heels, not by pressure on the reins. Rein pressure will not only cause a horse to dig its front end in, but it will also tend to make the horse attack the ground in an effort to stop quickly and so escape the rein pressure, rather than complete the stride and 'get into the ground' at the correct time.

Whether you are performing a flying change or a sliding stop, you must have the co-operation of your horse to do it well. This is particularly true in the case of the sliding stop. It simply is not possible to choose the exact stride on which to stop when travelling at nearly twenty-five miles per hour (40km per hour) down the arena. All the rider can do is suggest that it would be a good idea to stop, and let the horse do so at the time when it is best able, as it vaults over the leading leg. Such a response can only be achieved through a willing co-operation born of trust between horse and rider.

Speed Control on Circles

Most reining patterns require circles to be ridden at different speeds. So it is important that you practise controlling your speed on circles. Pay particular attention to keeping the circle round and the horse's body position correct. When riding faster you will find that your horse tends to be straighter through the body.

When increasing speed, you should not

Fig 122 Chasing Tewy in a controlled fast circle. Note that I have eased slightly forward in the saddle and run my rein hand up her neck.

Fig 123 The speed can be seen from the wind in her mane, but she is totally under control and only being guided by the hand.

Fig 124 Nicely balanced position of horse and rider working as a team.

urge your horse on with your legs. Instead, you should 'chase it up' by allowing your rein hand to move forward up the horse's neck, and by slightly inclining your body forward while pushing with a longer stroke of your seat. This will encourage your horse to lengthen its stride and step out. You should ride perhaps four circles at the faster speed and then, just when your horse is thinking about slowing down, you can take your rein hand back towards the saddle horn, maintaining a very light contact as you do so. Bring your body back to the vertical, sink your weight back into your seat (sack of potatoes style), and begin to shorten the length of your pelvic movement.

This will infallibly slow your horse down without you having to haul it back

with the reins. It may take a little while to begin with, but let the horse work out for itself what is going on on top. By both shortening your pelvic movement and raising it a little higher, you can encourage the horse to lift its back to correspond with your movements, rather than you corresponding with the horse. This has the effect of engaging the hindlegs more, moving the horse's centre of gravity back and slowing it down.

This may take a couple of laps of the circle the first few times you try it. Providing it works, however, then it is worth the wait because you will be producing a horse that responds to your seat and not solely to the reins. If your horse does not slow down within a reasonable time, you will have to put a little more weight on the reins to reinforce your

133

Fig 125 I have sat down more in the saddle, brought my body upright and dropped my hand back. The decrease in pace can be seen by the mane dropping flatter on her neck. The transition is relaxed and nicely controlled.

Fig 126 Compare this picture with the fast circle; you can see that she has collected herself and shortened her stride.

intentions. If you have done your basic schooling correctly, however, your horse should respond readily to your seat. Each time you repeat the exercise, the horse will come back to you a little sooner until eventually it will slow immediately it feels you change position.

This response to your seat and pelvic speed is crucial to establishing the smoothness of response you need in a reining horse. Whether you are building or reducing speed on your circles, it must never look rushed or jerky but smooth and controlled. This is only possible if you and your horse work together as a team.

10 Western Competition Classes

Many riders who begin Western riding start out convinced that they have no interest in competition. Often, however, it is not long before they are tempted to show off their new-found skills in the show ring. Among the various Western competition classes there is something for everyone. Even if you choose not to compete initially, the requirements of the various classes provide an excellent way for you to test your horse at home and add a little variety to its training programme.

Classes for Beginners

To encourage the widest participation in Western riding events, most Western competitions offer separate classes for novice horses and others for novice riders. For example, within the guidelines of the National Snaffle Bit Association, the Western Equestrian Society (the governing body of Western riding in the UK) has introduced the Arena Test A for riders wishing to enter Western Pleasure Classes. This event, which is very similar to Dressage Test 5, gives novice horses and riders the chance to perform the Pleasure Class paces individually in the show ring, before going into a class together with a number of other horses.

There is also a Novice Pleasure Class, which is intended for horses of any age ridden in a snaffle bit. This allows exist-ing horse owners the chance to compete on older horses which have perhaps only recently been reschooled to Western. Otherwise, the official National Snaffle Bit Association Novice Classes, and those of many others, are for horses of four years of age and younger.

Similarly, the Novice Trail Class is intended for newly trained or young horses ridden in a snaffle. These classes are not only intended to encourage people to enter the Western competitive scene, but also to continue training longer in the snaffle bit until the horse is fully finished and quite capable of working in the curb.

In the Western Riding Class, a further concession to novices is the Western Riding 'Simple' Class, where they are permitted to ride the course making simple changes of lead, rather than the flying changes which are mandatory in the Western Riding 'Flying' Class.

For those who wish to train for the Reining events, there is the Arena Test B. This test contains simpler reining manoeuvres, such as a gentle stop from the trot rather than a slide. This type of stop can also be done on grass where sliding would be dangerous.

So whether you or your horse are new to Western riding there is sure to be a class you can enter to demonstrate your teamwork and show off the results of your training.

The Western Pleasure Horse Class

The purpose of the Western Pleasure Horse Class is to show the smooth paces of the Western riding horse. All competitors enter the arena together and file around the edge at the walk. The judge will then ask the ring steward to call for the various paces of walk, jog and lope, in any sequence. He will also ask for a reversal, which is an inward turn to change the rein. (*See* Fig 78.)

The judge is looking for an obedient horse which responds promptly to the rider's aids. The judge is also looking for a horse that is well balanced and has a constant head carriage throughout the gaits and at the halt. Ideally, the judge wants to see a level topline throughout the test. It is quite permissible for the judge to ask for the jog to be extended into the trot. The judge wants to see a soft stride and low ground action. A horse which combines these qualities with good engagement and a balanced action will ride flat and so give the rider an easy, comfortable ride.

Throughout the test, the horse should be flexed at the poll, and the poll-wither-hip line should remain on a parallel. The judge also wants to see that the horse stays calm, despite having other horses around it, so that the rider needs very little rein contact to guide it around the arena. Anti-social behaviour such as flattening the ears or kicking will be severely penalised. The horses should also be able to rein back in a relaxed, easy manner, with no resistance, so that when the rider asks the horse to back, it simply melts in the poll, elevates its shoulders, drops its quarters and moves backwards.

Training for the Western Pleasure Class

When training for the Pleasure Class, emphasis must be placed on keeping your horse light, supple and obedient to your leg aids. Above all, you must be able to trust your horse to get on with the job, while being certain that it is listening to you at all times.

It is probably true to say that the Western Pleasure Class is the easiest event to enter but the hardest to win. A winning horse must perform like a metronome, yet be that contradiction in terms: a totally responsive and quiet horse which has character and presence. Achieving this effect takes a lot of training. The horse must be supple and athletic, but above all it must be quiet and responsive. One mistake you can make when training the pleasure horse is to ride aimlessly round and round your arena day after day. At best your horse will simply become bored and at worst it will begin to anticipate you and perhaps start taking decisions for itself.

It is vital, therefore, that you keep your training programme as varied as possible. Work through a few trail obstacles, for example, so that your horse always has something to concentrate on and remains attentive to your aids. That way, when you enter the show ring your horse will not feel that it knows what is coming next, but will listen to you and perform as required.

Two common faults, frequently seen in the Pleasure Class, are the rushing of upward transitions and a lack of engagement. In the Pleasure Class you must ride on a fairly slack rein. Consequently, there will always be the temptation for the poorly schooled horse to take liberties

Fig 127   Tewy demonstrating how little rein pressure you need to make a horse execute a perfect two-time rein back!

Fig 128 Giving the hip to the right.   *Fig 129 Giving the hip to the left.*

and accelerate when you ask it to step up into the jog or lope. So, in your schooling work with a little more contact and give and take with the reins and also concentrate on increasing engagement.

The soft Western paces must be achieved through greater engagement and suppleness, not by the horse falling asleep on its feet, or by you hauling it back with the reins. Regular practice of manoeuvres such as shoulder in, shoulder out, renvers, travers, direct and indirect bend circles, sidepassing and slow rollbacks, all encourage the horse to respond to your leg and shift its weight rearwards. Furthermore, the more supple the horse is, the better balanced it will be and the easier it will be able to do what we ask.

It is also useful to do some of your training around other horses so that your horse learns to concentrate on doing what you are telling it to do and not go copying the behaviour of its four-legged friends.

During the initial stages of your horse's training, you should allow it to walk, trot and canter on a loose rein at whatever pace it feels comfortable and balanced. As it finds its balance, you can begin to decrease its use of its head and neck as a balancing pole, by giving and taking with the reins. This will also help the horse to move its centre of gravity rearwards. You should also work on suppling exercises to make the horse soft in the poll, soft in the mouth and soft in the neck. This will enable your horse to bend while keeping its body upright. One of the commonest faults you will see in any poorly trained horse is a speeding up or breaking gait on corners, simply

139

because the horse has not been taught to give its shoulder and ribcage to the rider while flexing its head to the inside.

In its natural way of going, the horse would like to turn its head to the outside, drop its inside shoulder, lean into the corner and thereby lose its balance to the inside, whereupon its legs can scurry round to catch itself up. To ride a corner in a smooth balanced way, you must make your horse supple. You must persuade it to give its head and neck to the inside of a bend and so arc its body while keeping it upright. That way the horse will be able to continue moving more softly and maintain its rhythm. To encourage the horse to do this you must ensure that your aids are both strong and clear. Then, through repetition and the growing trust between you and your horse, you can work on making them imperceptible.

If you have no recourse to a 'groundman', when working on the Western gaits of jog and lope, it is a good idea to school your horse in the round pen from time to time. From your position on the ground you can make certain that your horse maintains engagement in the slower paces. You can always spot horses which have been 'reined' slower because they leave their legs behind them and there is no roundness to their loins; as soon as the rider gives with the reins, the horse falls onto its forehand and starts to speed up again.

You must remember that the soft engaged stride is actually quite difficult for a horse and is also quite tiring. Once you have achieved the pace you desire for a short while, allow your horse to rest. If you intersperse your circle work with slow rollbacks at trot and canter, you will also help the horse to engage deeper. This technique has always been part of Western training and is now finding favour with a few top show jumpers, who have equal need for increased engagement, albeit for a different purpose.

A simple test you can perform to see how well your horse is progressing, is to ride a forty-foot (12 m) circle and see whether your horse can manage to keep its shoulder up and its ribcage square. At the same time, you should also be able to pick up on either rein and flex your horse's head towards your toe while its body continues on the same line of the circle. If at any time your horse starts to speed up or resist, then you know you have more work to do.

A winning Pleasure Class horse should be the horse that, at the end of the day, you would pick out as the one you would most like to ride because it looks the smoothest and lightest and is therefore a real pleasure to ride.

The Trail Class

The Trail Class is probably the competition which is most applicable to our everyday riding. It is a test to show not only that the horse is able to negotiate obstacles calmly and obediently without getting into a stew, but also to show off the soft, relaxed paces of the Western horse.

Ideally, the rider should simply present the obstacle to the horse, give the go ahead to do it, and the horse should then just proceed with the job. Between the obstacles, the rider should demonstrate the three gaits of walk, jog and lope, as requested by the judges. Obviously no competition can contain all the obstacles one might meet out on a hack. Instead, a course is constructed containing the most common hazards, together with trials which test the horse's obedience to the aids.

There are three mandatory tests in any Trail Class: the gate, the logs and the L-shaped rein back. Whatever else is added is up to the course designer. A typical Trail Class might also include poles which must be sidepassed over, a bridge to cross, scary objects which must be carried, noisy, colourful clothing which must be put on and taken off, turns in tight boxes and raised poles which must be stepped over – all hazards which might be encountered out on a ride.

Clearly, before you can consider entering a Trail Class, you must have a horse that can sidepass, turn on its haunches, turn on its forehand, rein back and step over obstacles with its head down to see where it is placing its feet.

I include basic Trail Class tests early on in a young horse's training for no other reason than to ensure that the horse is safe and responsive out on a hack. If each of the various obstacles is introduced to the horse over a period of time, first with the rider at the horse's side and leading, and then later mounted, the horse will learn not to fear the unusual and always to trust the rider's commands. Older horses can also benefit from this approach, particularly if they suffer from the frights. On a more sensible older horse, however, you may feel that you can begin your training from the saddle.

When introducing a new obstacle or test, it is a good idea to ride up to it slowly and then stop. Allow the horse time to have a good look at it from all angles and to pick up on your relaxed manner. That way the horse will learn that this new object is not something to fear. Once

your horse is perfectly relaxed, you can quietly ride it over, round or through the obstacle, taking your time and stopping every few paces or so to accustom your horse to this new experience. Once you have completed an obstacle, do not rush away from it or your horse might get the idea that it is something to escape from.

This softly, softly approach will teach your horse to stay quiet and calm, and a calm horse is a thinking horse. As you begin to train your horse more seriously to negotiate the various tests, be patient. Even if your horse keeps making mistakes, never punish or discipline it in the middle of an obstacle or you run the risk of establishing bad associations. Walk the horse away and then try again.

The Gate

The correct way to tackle a gate in a Trail Class is to sidepass up to it and stand and relax at the latch end. You should then reach down, unlatch the gate and rein your horse back so its nose is clear of the latch post. Open the gate with your hand and push your horse through with a turn on the haunches. Ride through the opening while sliding your hand along the top rail of the gate without letting go.

Once through, halt your horse, then turn it on the forehand so that its hindquarters clear the gate post. Bring the gate past your leg then complete another turn on the haunches, sliding your hand back up the gate, whereupon you should find yourself perfectly positioned to be able to relatch it. You should then rest there for a moment so that your horse remains attentive and will not start thinking that the obstacle should be rushed.

Bridge and Poles

When negotiating obstacles such as the bridge or poles, you should walk over them cleanly, without your horse tripping or banging them. To do this you need to train your horse to look down, so that it knows exactly where to put its feet.

The best way to teach your horse to look down is to stop before an obstacle, lean forwards slightly, placing more weight in the stirrups, and give away the reins. The combined effect of something strange at its feet, your weight transference and the freedom of no rein contact should encourage the horse to look down. Some trainers put sugar lumps on the obstacles while others tap the horse lightly on the head. Whatever way you do it, be sure to praise your horse as soon as it lowers its head correctly. Soon it will begin to associate the stop and long rein as an invitation to look down and be praised.

If your horse does kick an obstacle, do not punish it or start hauling it about with the reins. Simply reposition the poles and do the test again. You must trust your horse and work on the assumption that it would prefer to step cleanly through the obstacle than bruise its legs. All you can do is encourage it to look and then to help it through the obstacle by giving it a long rein and sitting as still and quietly as you can.

L-shaped Rein Back

The L-shaped rein back is another of the required elements of the Trail Class. It is designed to show that your horse will not only step backwards quietly, accurately and under full control, but also that you can turn your horse while backing.

When training for this manoeuvre, take plenty of time. Line your horse up very precisely with the poles to give yourself the best possible chance of completing the obstacle cleanly. Then rein back one step at a time and, at least to begin with, rest after every step. Your horse should automatically stand square, and, by stopping after each step, it will not be tempted to rush back and make mistakes.

If you do begin to go off line slightly, apply a little gentle leg pressure to the side that is slipping out. Overcorrection is the most common fault here, with the result that you fishtail your way through the obstacle, crashing out first one side and then the other. The slower you move, however, the easier you will find it to stay straight.

When you reach the turn, begin to sink a little weight into your outside seatbone, and take a little extra feel of the outside rein. Ease the horse's hind end round, taking care it does not step out with its front end. Again, do not try to complete the turn in one go but edge round a little at a time. Do this by applying a little leg pressure and then, as your horse begins to step round, remove your leg. That way the horse will still take the step but it should then stop.

If you negotiate any obstacle in this way, you will always know where you are and what, if anything, needs to be done to stay on course. Once round the turn, make sure you are perfectly straight again before completing the rein back. Another common mistake is to feel so relieved at having completed the turn that you rush to complete the obstacle, excite your horse and make a mistake.

Fig 130 Negotiating the L-shaped rein back: after a slow and steady back up, the horse's quarters should be turned in a relaxed manner.

Fig 131 Once the horse is completely square, begin backing once more.

*Fig 132   Bob Mayhew performing an L-shaped back up
in the Trail Class.*

The Sidepass

Before sidepassing along poles it is important that you first align yourself perfectly and then stop and relax your horse. Once in position, by putting your weight into one seatbone and leg, while removing the contact from the other, you should be able to push your horse sideways along the pole.

As you do this you must take up just enough rein contact to prevent your horse from taking a step forward, but not so much contact that it steps back. Judging the right amount of feel can only come with practice.

Carrying Objects

Practice is also the key to accustoming your horse to tests such as picking up a sack of cans from one barrel, carrying them on your back and then dropping them into another barrel. As these classes get tougher, and the horses more relaxed and bombproof, in order to win it is not good enough simply to 'survive' the test. You must perform it with a little extra flair.

In this case, you might sidepass up to the barrel, whisk the sack into the air, bounce it on your horse's back, move off at the lope, come to a quiet halt, sidepass

Fig 133 Negotiating a T-shaped side pass: Sheila begins this manoeuvre with her weight in her right seatbone and applying right leg pressure. She balances the horse's body with just enough rein contact to stop it from walking forward, but not so much as to make it step back.

145

Fig 134 *Arriving at the centre of the T, Sheila makes a turn on the haunches, taking the horse's front end through the gap before continuing the sidepass. Sheila then takes the horse back to the gap, applying left seatbone weight and leg pressure.*

Fig 135 *At the gap, Sheila draws her left leg back a touch, taking the horse's haunches through the gap.*

Fig 136 Sheila continues to apply left leg and seatbone pressure, and Keo continues to sidepass to the end of the obstacle in a calm, relaxed manner.

up to the barrel and slam the cans in. Such a display would demonstrate without question that your horse is not only relaxed and completely untroubled by strange, noisy objects, but that it is still 100 per cent awake and responsive to your aids.

The Turnaround

The turnaround, in a marked-out box only just longer than the horse, requires a combination of skills. First your horse must look where it is going and step into the box without kicking the poles. Then it must combine a turn on the forehand with a turn on the haunches, so that it rotates about its centre, without stepping forwards or backwards.

This is another trail test that is genuinely practical. If you found yourself stuck on a narrow path with obstacles such as parked cars around you, then you would need to turn round in a quiet and accurate manner so as not to excite your horse and end up damaging the cars. Again, the secret is to teach your horse to take small quiet steps to the side and not step backwards or forwards. Throughout the turn you should stop frequently and rest your horse to keep it calm.

When you have completed the turn, you should let the horse rest. Then, when you are ready, you can pitch the reins away, put a little weight in your stirrups and lean forward. Your horse should then lower its head, look at the pole, and step over it carefully as it leaves the box.

Fig 137 The turnaround in a small box: the horse has to complete the 360-degree turn without touching the sides.

Western Riding Class

The Western Riding Class was originally established by the late Monte Foreman to show off the calm paces of the working ranch horse. This class is based on the very practical skills required of a horse working cattle over a variety of terrain.

For a horse to work cattle properly it must be well balanced, always on the correct lead and able to move quietly in a relaxed manner at all times and in all paces. It must also be able to negotiate the most frequently encountered obstacles – gates and fallen trees. All these requirements have been combined to produce the Western Riding Class.

At the entrance to the arena there will be a gate which you should negotiate in the same way as for the Trail Class. You then walk down the long side of the arena and step cleanly over a log. When you have cleared the log, you must pick up a jog, and ride the remainder of the long side and half-way round the short side, at which point you should pick up a lope on the left lead.

Along the next long side there will be five equally spaced marker cones set out between thirty and forty-five feet (10 and 15m) apart. You should ride through the cones, changing leads precisely between each of them, and so demonstrating four flying changes. You then continue the lope around the other short side and past the gate. You will then face three equally spaced cones, through which again you must weave, riding backwards and forwards across the arena, changing leads each time you cross the centre of the arena. You must lope over the log once, and finish with a lope down the centre line, an easy halt and a calm, relaxed rein back.

Western Riding offers a little bit of everything and is the favourite event of many Western riders. Training for this class requires work on all aspects of your riding, from the basic paces, to negotiating trail obstacles and the ability to master flying changes.

Reining

Reining is arguably the highest form of competitive Western riding. It is effectively a high speed dressage test incorporating key Western manoeuvres such as the rollback, the spin and sliding stop. In open classes it must be ridden one-handed with the horse in a curb bit, although there are classes for young horses ridden in a snaffle bit or bosal. For obvious reasons, therefore, Reining should only be attempted by finished horses trained to a high standard.

There are nine National Reining Horse Association and seven American Quarter Horse Association Reining patterns, any one of which might be selected for a competition. Each pattern is scored from 60 to 80, with 70 being an average score. There are fixed penalties for delayed lead changes, over-spins and other technical faults.

In the NRHA Judges' guide, reining is neatly summed up as follows:

> To rein a horse is not merely to guide him, but to also control his every movement. The best reined horse should be wilfully guided or controlled with little or no apparent resistance and dictated to completely. Any movement on his own must be considered a lack of control. All deviations from the exact written pattern must be considered a lack of or temporary loss of control; and therefore a fault that must be marked down according to the severity of deviation. After deducting all faults … credit should be given for smoothness, finesse, attitude, quickness and authority of performing various manoeuvres, while using controlled speed which raises the difficulty level and makes him more exciting and pleasing to watch to an audience.

Illustrated is NRHA Pattern 5 (*see* Fig 138), which gives a good idea of the requirements of a typical Reining test and how the various manoeuvres are linked together. This pattern should be run as follows:

Begin at the centre of the arena facing the left wall or fence. Begin on the left lead and complete two circles to the left. The first one large and fast, the second one small and slow.

At the centre of the arena stop and

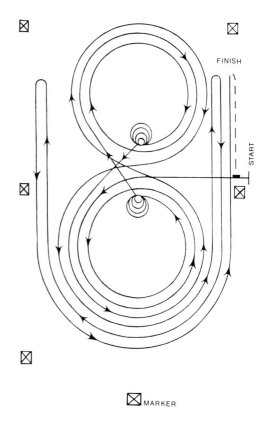

Fig 138 Reining pattern 5.

complete four spins to the left, so that you end up facing the wall. Then hesitate. Taking the right lead, complete two circles to the right, the first one large and fast, the second one small and slow.

Stop in the centre again and complete four spins to the right so you end up facing the left wall. Then hesitate.

Taking the left lead, ride a figure of eight over the large circles. Close the figure of eight and begin a large fast circle to the left. Do not close this circle but run straight down the side, past the centre marker and do a right rollback at least twenty-one feet (7m) from the wall or fence without hesitating.

149

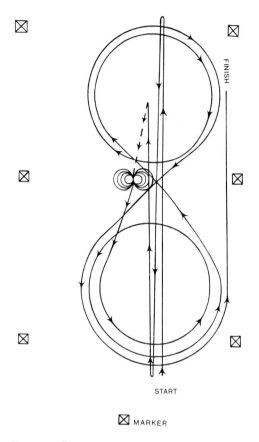

Fig 139 Reining pattern 1.

circle but do not close the circle. Run straight down the side, past the centre marker and do a sliding stop at least twenty-one feet (7m) from the fence. Back up over your slide tracks for a minimum of nine feet (3m).

Finally, hesitate to demonstrate the completion of the pattern and then drop the bridle to the judge.

That is how the pattern shapes up from the rider's point of view. As far as the judges are concerned, it breaks down into eight manoeuvres and the same scores apply to each. It is important to note that the fast large, slow small circle combinations count just as much as the rundown, stop and rollback. So never get too excited about a thirty-foot (10m) slide (well, not too excited!), it is a good overall performance that will win the day. The important thing is always to make the pattern flow accurately and calmly, something which only comes with training, and relaxed training at that.

As you can appreciate from this example, Reining tests every aspect of a horse and rider's performance. Training therefore requires far more than the mastery of individual manoeuvres, in that you must work towards putting them together in a smooth and seamless performance.

Continue back around the previous circle but do not close the circle. Instead run down the other side past the centre marker and do a left rollback at least twenty-one feet (7m) from the fence without hesitating.

Continue back around the previous

150

Appendix 1

The Importance of a Training Programme

Whether you ride purely for pleasure or desire to compete at the highest level, it is important that you always ride with purpose. Much bad or sloppy riding can be traced directly to the rider's aimlessness. By continually setting yourself, and your horse, new goals to achieve, not only will you enjoy your riding more but, at the end of the day, you will be a better rider as well.

Throughout this book I have tried to stress the fact that schooling is not something to be left exclusively to gifted instructors, or something which should only take place in riding schools and arenas. Perhaps if we used a different word, such as training or guiding, it would be easier for riders to accept that it is something they should do themselves every time they visit their horse, tack it up and ride it out.

Probably the best way to keep the importance of this approach uppermost in your mind, is to keep a diary of your achievements. For a young horse, the whole training programme can be mapped out from scratch. Older horses can first be assessed, and then you can invent a programme that concentrates on the areas in which your horse performs least well.

Initial Requirements

Your first requirements of the young or green horse is that it can be led in a head collar or bosal and will stop and stand square on command. The horse should be able to rein back, turn on the forehand and the haunches and sidepass.

You should also concentrate on flexion exercises, so that, with your horse stationary, you can lift the slack out of either rein and the horse will give its nose without resistance. If you repeat this exercise a few times every time you take your horse out, it will soon develop such a supple head and neck that when you ride it you will be able to touch your boot with its nose – without turning its shoulders or moving from the halt. If the shoulders do move, you know the horse is not sufficiently supple for advanced work.

In the first four months of training you should extend the programme to include direct and indirect bend circles and reinbacks in a circle, all at the walk, so that the horse learns to give its hip. For variety, you can also introduce the horse to a wide range of obstacles, and ride it at a trot.

During the next four months you should develop all the basics so that they can be performed at the trot and the canter. You should also be working on developing greater flexion and teaching your horse to respond to a lighter contact. Within the first twelve months your horse should be able to perform a good Trail Class test in a snaffle bit without making mistakes. It should also be able to perform all the Western paces in a more than reasonable manner.

Transitions to jog and lope should be smooth and the horse should hold the gait until asked to break down. At the lope and canter your horse should pick up the correct lead reliably. It should stop square and get its hocks well underneath it. At this stage you should also have the beginnings of the turnaround. In other words, your horse should be able to cope with walking a very small circle with its nose tipped to the inside, while staying upright in its body. This will sharpen the turn on the haunches and forehand. Overall the horse should now be becoming very light in the bridle.

In the following six to twelve months you should polish all these exercises to a high standard. You should be able to sidepass at canter and jog without speeding up. You should be able to ride on an ultra-light contact at all times. Provided your horse has coped with all its training so far and is enjoying its work, at this point you can consider introducing it to the shanked snaffle or Billy Allen snaffle and go on to develop the basis of neck reining. The horse should now become even lighter still.

As you work towards a finished horse you should be striving for perfection in everything you do. Your horse should now accept the curb bit and understand neck reining completely. It should also be capable of the more advanced techniques such as fast spins, lead changes every five strides and sliding stops if you are Reining.

From then on, how far you go will depend on both your skill and the ability of your horse, but your training should never stop. There is always more to learn and, however close you get, perfection is always a stride or two away. Nonetheless you will end up with a horse that is a lot more fun to ride, and when all is said and done, surely that is what it is all about.

Glossary

barrel the body of a horse between hips and shoulders.

bars the part of the horse's mouth, between the incisor and molar teeth, on which the bit rests, or, part of the saddle tree which holds the stirrup leathers.

billet the two ends of the rear cinch.

bosal round nose band of braided rawhide, also known as a hackamore, but not to be confused with a mechanical hackamore.

cantle the rear (usually raised) part of a saddle's seat.

collection the act of training a horse to bring its hindlegs well under it and to flex at the poll so that its centre of gravity is further back, in order to lighten its forehand.

cinch alternative name for girth.

cow-hocked a horse so conformed that its hocks are closer together than its stifles or pasterns.

croup highest point of a horse's hips.

curb bit a bit which employs mechanical leverage and applies pressure via the curb strap under the chin.

cut, cutting to separate a single animal, usually a cow, from a herd.

dishing the act of tipping the front feet outwards as they are lifted for each step.

disunited a canter, lope or gallop where the horse leads with a leg on one side at the front and on the other side at the rear.

eggbutt a type of snaffle bit.

fender large flap of leather attached to the stirrups, designed to protect the rider's legs from the sweat of the horse.

fiador a brow band and throatlatch, seldom used today, made of knotted rope and designed to hold a bosal in place.

fork front arch of the saddle to which the horn is attached.

grazing bit a low-ported curb bit with short, curved shanks.

hackamore an English corruption of the Spanish *jaquima*, used to describe a bitless bridle, *not* to be confused with mechanical varieties.

headstall a bridle minus the bit.

jog trot a very slow trot.

latigo the strap which attaches the cinch to the saddle rigging.

lead in canter and lope a horse leads with the forefoot which touches the ground independently of its other feet.

lope a slow canter.

mecate a traditional hair rope used as a lead rope and reins with a bosal. Usually about twenty feet (7 m) long and tied with a special knot.

neck rein the technique of directing a horse by applying pressure to the side of the neck.

paddling the action of turning the hoof outwards as the foot is raised to take a step.

port the central, upwardly curved section of a curb bit.

quirt whip

reverse an inward, small, 180-degree turn from walk or jog used to change direction in a Pleasure Class.

rollback a stop, reverse and change of leads performed from the lope.

romal an extension to joined reins, which can be used as a quirt.

rowel the wheel on a spur.

shank sidepiece of a curb bit.

sidepass a sideways movement, with the horse's legs crossing in front and behind.

snaffle a type of bit which works on a 1:1 ratio on the corners of a horse's mouth. It may be jointed or solid.

spade a traditional, high-ported and often fancy bit that is, in the wrong hands, extremely severe.

spin also called a turnaround, a fast 360-degree turn, or series of turns, on the hindquarters, with the inside pivot foot staying planted in the same position throughout.

stirrup leathers leather straps which support the stirrups.

two-track to travel with the horse's body at an angle to the direction of motion.

Useful Addresses

Western Equestrian Society
Mrs B Carder
65 Wealdbridge Road
Northweald
Essex CM16 6ES

**National Reining Horse
  Association of Great Britain**
Ann Pearsons
Burnt Ash
Sheep Street Lane
Etchingham
East Sussex TN19 7AY

British Quarter Horse Association
4th Street
National Agricultural Centre
Stoneleigh Park
Kenilworth
Warwickshire CV8 2LG

The British Appaloosa Society
Mr and Mrs Howkins
c/o 2 Frederick Street
Rugby
Warwickshire CV21 2EN

British Palomino Society
Penrhiwllan
Llanddysul
Dyfed SA44 5NZ

**The Coloured Horse and Pony
  Society**
Miss Penelope Shephard
15 Wilga Road
Welwyn A16 9PT

**American Quarter Horse
  Association**
PO Box 32470
2701 1-40 East
Amarillo
Texas 79120
USA

**National Reining Horse
  Association**
28881 SR83
Coshocton
OH 43812
USA

Index

Italic numerals denote page numbers of illustrations.